The Father of Modern India
WILLIAM CAREY

Vishal and Ruth Mangalwadi

In honour of Western Missionaries
who loved the Indian subcontinent enough
to serve with little recognition or gratitude

The Father of Modern India—William Carey

Published by Sought After Media
1077 N Willow Ave., Ste 105 PMB 1010, Clovis, CA 93611-4411 USA
Manager@SoughtAfterMedia.com 323-202-9307
Outside the USA distributed by www.Triaze.com

ISBN 979-8-9887831-0-7

This is a revised, expanded version of the book first published in 1993 by Nivedit Good Books Distributors Private Ltd., under the title *William Carey: A Tribute by an Indian Woman* and then as *William Carey and the Regeneration of India.*

In 1997, OM Publishing brought out a revised version in the United Kingdom as *Carey, Christ and Cultural Transformation.* Crossway Books, a division of Good News Publishers, Wheaton, Illinois USA published the 1999, edition as *The Legacy of William Carey* with a Study Guide © by Darrow L. Miller.

CONTENTS

Preface

〰〰〰

THE FATHER OF MODERN INDIA?

Some Indians think that Mahatma Gandhi is the Father of Modern India. However, no national forum has ever conferred that honour upon the Mahatma.

It is said that Netaji Subhash Chandra Bose first called Mahatma Gandhi "the father of the nation" in 1944, in a radio broadcast from Singapore. Bose spoke as a politician, not as a historian. His objective was to undermine Gandhi's hold upon Indian imagination: specifically, the Mahatma's principle of non-violence (*Ahimsa*). Bose was motivating Indian soldiers serving Britain, to revolt against the British Raj, team up with Adolf Hitler, and militarily overthrow colonialism.

Four years later, when a militant Hindu assassinated Mahatma Gandhi, India's first Prime Minister, Pandit Jawaharlal Nehru, re-echoed Bose's sentiment. His objective was to honour his mentor. Serious historians, however, have made the case that Nehru's influence upon India (for better or for worse) has been greater than Mahatma Gandhi's.

When we were growing up, our history teachers said that Raja Ram Mohan Roy (1772-1833) was the 'Father of Modern India.' Younger Indians no longer believe that. Many Hindutva scholars hate Roy because his reform agenda came from William Carey.

"Upper" caste Hindus find it very difficult to admit that a British *chamar* (a "low" caste cobbler)-turned-Bible translator, who never studied in a university, is the father of modern India.

Carey arrived in Bengal in 1793 as a fugitive. It was because the British Parliament banned missionaries from going to Bengal, the eastern part of the Mughal Empire, administered by the British East India Comapny. It included present-day Bangladesh, Assam, Odisha, and Bihar.

The British Parliament had the authority to ban missionaries because in 1765, the Mughal Emperor had given Bengal's administrative authority (*Diwani*) to the British East India Company. William Carey and his fellow missionaries had to open their mission in Serampore, thirty kilometers north of Calcutta (now Kolkata) because it was a Danish territory.

Before Carey settled in Serampore, around 1796–97, a Sanskrit scholar, Tantric Hariharananda Vidyabagish, had taken Raja Ram Mohan Roy to William Carey to learn English and teach Sanskrit. The three of them co-authored a book on Hindu law, *Maha Nirvana Tantra* (or *The Book of the Great Liberation*).

Indologist William Jones had already translated *Manusmriti* (or *Laws of Manu*) into English in 1794. However, hardly anyone knew what the *Manusmriti* said. No one treated it as the Hindu equivalent of Muslim *Sharia,* Jewish Torah, or the English Common Law. Since *Manusmriti* was never used as the basis for resolving legal disputes among Hindus, some British judges began using *The Book of the Great Liberation* as the only "Hindu law" available to them at that time.

Raja Ram Mohan Roy returned to Carey in Serampore in about 1820. By 1812 he had begun to dislike widow-burning when his sister-in-law committed Sati. William Carey attracted him because he had already researched the practice and written against it. Carey's compassionate research gave Roy the rationale for opposing widow-burning. Additionally, the Baptist mission helped Roy understand why the sixteenth-century Protestant Reformation had transformed medieval Europe into modern.

The time Ram Mohan spent in Serampore helped him reject polytheism (many gods) and embrace monotheism (one God). The world is so filled with evil that everyone and everything cannot be god. Human sin can be judged only if there is one God who is good. The world can be reformed only by a God who is above the world, who transcends it. Roy realised that God's children should not worship stones and snakes, monkeys and mountains, human gurus and evil spirits. We ought to establish our dominion over nature. We must make sure that our Father's will is done on earth, including through science and technology.

The early nineteenth century was a time when Rationalism was making it difficult for Western theologians to accept the Trinity—that one God existed in three persons: Father, Son, and the Holy Spirit. Unitarianism was taking over Christian universities. Therefore, while Roy was translating the Gospel of John along with a Scottish missionary, William Adam, the two of them became Unitarians.

William Adam resigned from Serampore Mission. In September 1821, they established Calcutta's Unitarian Society. Later, in 1828, Roy established its indigenous version, the Brahmo Samaj. It was a quasi-Christian sect which rejected the authority of the Vedas, idol worship, belief in Hindu avatars (incarnations of deities), and karma/reincarnation. The Samaj discarded brahminical rituals, championed monotheism, and followed William Carey's approach to social reform.

* * *

Ruth and I self-published the original version of this book in 1993 to celebrate the bicentennial of Carey's arrival in India. At that time we did not realise that William Carey was the 'Father of Modern India.'

In 1994, Arun Shourie's attack on Christian missions, motivated me to go beyond Carey to study how Christian missions impacted India during the nineteenth century. My letters to Arun Shourie became the book, *Missionary Conspiracy: Letters to a Postmodern Hindu*.

When India began celebrating the golden jubilee of her independence, my research expanded into the Bible's impact upon India during the twentieth century. Out of that came the 1997 book, *India: The Grand Experiment*. It presented the thesis that India's freedom was a fruit of the Gospel and that rejecting the Gospel was propelling India towards fascism. By 1997, India had already corrupted the history of its freedom. Many Indians had embraced ancient myths along with fascist ideology. Consequently, India was sliding from freedom into authoritarianism.

The insight that modern India was born as a result of what William Carey began along with his friends, followers, and successors dawned on me when I began reflecting upon Mr. Rajiv Malhotra's book, *Breaking India*. The last chapter of this volume explains how Mr. Malhotra enlightened me.

The first American edition of our book on Carey was published to celebrate the bicentennial of the founding of his Serampore Mission— the first Protestant mission from the English-speaking world to the non-English-speaking world.

This edition celebrates the 75th anniversary of India's independence. In the months ahead we plan to publish a series titled *How The Bible Created Modern India*. It is being co-authored with 30 or so researchers.

India is still independent, but it has already lost much of its freedom. Before it becomes fully fascist, we need to learn from reformers such as William Carey. His mind (worldview) and methods remain a source of light in today's darkness.

Carey, his colleagues, and successors transformed the fragmented and oppressive Mughal India by loving people while battling wrong ideas. They did not fight individual politicians or communities but served God and India.

In his classic study, *South Asia: A Short History* (Macmillan, 1989), historian Hugh Tinker summed up the essence of Carey's method and its results:

> "And so in Serampore, on the banks of river Hooghly, soon after 1800, the principal elements in Modern South Asia, popular linguistic identification ("linguism"), the press, the university, social consciousness—all came to light. The West and South Asia were about to come to grips with each other in terms not merely of power and profit, but also of ideas and principles."

Carey's life can help us shape our future.

Vishal Mangalwadi,
April 14, 2023

FOREWORD TO THE 1999 EDITION

Dr. Ralph D. Winter

THIS BOOK CONFIRMS IN A DELIGHTFUL, page-turning drama a series of events that reasonably could be considered the least likely to have happened. It is the story of a young man with almost no formal education, from a small town, speaking the wrong dialect, losing all his hair in childhood illness, yet uncovering high purpose in a far-off land... where he was constantly harassed by colonial functionaries, deserted by his armchair mission leaders back home, misunderstood and opposed by the younger recruits sent out to help him, buffeted by colossal setbacks, and yet, without trying, becoming perhaps the most influential person in the largest outpost of the British Empire.

It is truly staggering to realise, as Vishal and Ruth Mangalwadi reveal in these pages, how the work of a single person was responsible for so much of the enormous cultural transformation that transpired on the massive Indian subcontinent in the nineteenth and twentieth centuries. Not only that, but India's future hinges as much on that contribution as has its past. How in the world could this have happened? In this small book you will find in compact, readable form the "truth stranger than fiction" behind this amazing, tragic, heroic story.

This is not, however, simply a brief account of one man's story. It is the untying of a knot of enormous complexity, the mystery of the great influence of small things on a billion wonderful people. While India is roughly just one-third the size of the "lower forty-eight" United States, its population is more than three times as great. Yet few people have left as large an imprint on that great nation as has William Carey. You can think of Mother Teresa in Calcutta. But in a way she was building on Carey in a city where, until recent years, the largest daily newspaper, The Statesman, proclaimed in its masthead that it was founded by William Carey.

Today many have followed in Carey's footsteps to virtually every corner of the earth. Individually, they may have his courage, his selflessness, even his dedication. But few have his strikingly wide spectrum of sensitivities to the basic issues confronting true gospel witness in this world. Some detractors say we would never have heard of William Carey had it not been for his missionary colleagues Joshua Marshman and William Ward. That is like saying we would never have heard of Napoleon had he not had an army behind him. Napoleon created his army; and Marshman and Ward would not even have been in India except for William Carey. They would not have stayed with him had he not been worthy of their faithfulness. His career is not one of "lucking out" again and again. It is almost the reverse. It is one of again and again surmounting "unlucky" major setbacks, and standing on them in humble victory.

Parallels are at hand. We think of the many obstacles and draining experiences the apostle Paul faced, and rightly wonder at his incalculable influence. Or if you want to note the impact of another lad from a small, despised town on the very fringes of social respectability, consider Jesus of Nazareth.

This book is in a sense merely the continuation of the story of God's miraculous work-work that is often opposed and misunderstood, but which as the centuries unfold is clearly the controlling voice in human history. The authors of this book are carrying that work forward in their own lives and writings.

Many know about William Carey. Few understand as do the Mangalwadis the profound contemporary significance of his life. We are deeply indebted to them for rescuing William Carey from the mere drama of his lifetime. Will we let them help us see beyond the mere drama of our own lives?

Ralph D. Winter,
Chancellor, William Carey International University,
Pasadena, California – January, 1999

Chapter One

A QUIZ: WHO WAS WILLIAM CAREY?

IMAGINE A QUIZMASTER AT THE FINALS of the All India Universities General Knowledge competition. He asks the best-informed Indian students, "Who was William Carey?" All hands go up simultaneously.

CHRISTIAN MISSIONARY AND BOTANIST

"William Carey was a Christian missionary," answers a science student. "And he was also the self-taught botanist after whom *Careya herbacea* is named. It is one of the three varieties of eucalyptus found only in India."

Carey brought the English daisy to India and introduced the Linnaean system to gardening. He also published the first books on science and natural history in India, such as William Roxburgh's *Flora Indica*, because he believed the Bible's view that, 'All Thy works praise Thee, O Lord.' Carey believed that nature is declared 'good' by its Creator; it is not *maya* (illusion), to be shunned, but a subject worthy of human study. He frequently lectured on science and tried to show that even lowly insects are not souls in bondage, but creatures worthy of our attention."

INDUSTRIALIST

"William Carey introduced the steam engine to India," pipes up a student of mechanical engineering. "And he was the first to make indigenous paper for our publishing industry. He encouraged Indian blacksmiths to make copies of his engine using local materials and skills."

ECONOMIST

"William Carey," announces an economics major, "introduced the idea of savings banks to India, to fight the all-pervasive social evil of usury. The Bible taught Carey that God, being righteous, hated usury, and that lending at interest rates of 36 to 72 percent made investment, industry, commerce, and economic development impossible.

"The moral dimensions of Carey's economic efforts," the student continues, "have assumed special importance in India, since the trustworthiness of the savings banks has become questionable due to the greed and corruption of the bankers and the nationalisation of the banks in the name of socialism. The all-pervasive culture of bribery has, in many cases, pushed the interest rates up to as much as 100 percent and made credit unavailable to honest entrepreneurs, and forced economists to rethink their separation of economics from morality.

"In order to attract European capital to India and to modernise Indian agriculture, economy, and industry, Carey also advocated the policy of allowing Europeans to own land and property in India. Initially, the British government was against such a policy because of its questionable results in the United States. But by the time of Carey's death, the same government had acknowledged the far-reaching economic wisdom of his stand—just as our Indian government today, after a half-century of destructive xenophobia, has again opened the doors for Western capital and industry."

MEDICAL HUMANITARIAN

"William Carey," asserts a medical student, "was the first to campaign for the humane treatment of India's leprosy patients. Until his time they were sometimes buried or burned alive because of the belief that a violent end purified the body and ensured transmigration into a healthy new existence. Natural death by disease was believed to result in four successive births, followed by a fifth birth as a leper. Carey believed that Jesus' love touches leprosy patients, so they should be cared for."

MEDIA PIONEER

A student of print technology stands up next. "Dr. William Carey is the father of print technology in India. He brought us the modern science of printing and publishing, then taught and developed it. His missionary community built what was then the largest press in India. Most printers bought their fonts from his Mission Press at Serampore."

"William Carey," responds a student of mass communications, "established the first newspaper ever printed in any oriental language, because he believed that, 'Above all forms of truth and faith, Christianity seeks free discussion.' His English language journal, *Friend of India*, was the force that gave birth to the social reform movement in India in the first half of the nineteenth century. It continues today as *The Statesman*, published from Calcatta."

AGRICULTURIST

"William Carey founded India's Agri-Horticultural Society in the 1820s, thirty years before the Royal Agricultural Society was established in England," says a postgraduate student of agriculture. "Carey did a systematic survey of agriculture in India, campaigned for agriculture reform in the journal *Asiatic Researches*, and exposed the evils of the indigo cultivation system two generations before it collapsed.

"Carey did all this," adds the agriculturist, "not because he was hired to do it, but because he was horrified to see that India's otherworldly spirituality had allowed three-fifths of one of the finest countries in the world, full of industrious inhabitants, to become an uncultivated jungle abandoned to wild beasts and serpents. Carey's attempt to transform Indian agriculture inspired the evangelical movement to build dams, irrigation canals, institutions to teach agriculture, horticulture and scientific animal husbandry. That movement climaxed in the Green Revolution of the 1960s."

TRANSLATOR AND EDUCATOR

"Carey began India's linguistic revolution transforming oral dialects into literary languages that could educate the masses," says a student of literature. "In his day, Persian was India's court language, even though not even Muslims spoke Persian. Moghul emperors had promoted Persian as a language of discrimination, just as the Indian elite promoted Sanskrit to keep the masses away from knowledge. Carey was the first to translate and publish in English great Indian religious classics such as the *Ramayana* and philosophical treatises such as *Samkhya*. Carey transformed Bengali, previously considered 'fit only for demons and women' into the foremost literary language of India. He wrote gospel ballads in Bengali to bring the Hindu love of musical recitations to the service of his Lord. He also wrote the first Sanskrit dictionary for scholars."

"Carey was a British cobbler," joins in a student of education, "who became a professor of Bengali, Sanskrit, and Marathi at Fort William College in Calcutta, where civil servants were trained. Carey's mission began dozens of schools for Indian children of all castes, and launched the first college in Asia, at Serampore near Calcutta. His motive was to develop the Indian mind and liberate it from the darkness of superstition. For nearly three thousand years, India's religious culture had denied most Indians free access to knowledge; and the Hindu,

Mughal, and British rulers had gone along with this high-caste strategy of keeping the masses in the bondage of ignorance. Carey displayed enormous spiritual strength in standing against the priests, who had a vested interest in depriving the masses of the freedom and power that come from the knowledge of the truth."

ASTRONOMER

"William Carey introduced the study of astronomy to the Subcontinent," declares a student of mathematics. "He was deeply concerned about the destructive cultural ramifications of astrology: fatalism, superstitious fear, and an inability to organise and manage time."

"Carey wanted to introduce India to the scientific culture of astronomy. He did not believe that the heavenly bodies were 'deities that governed our lives.' He knew that human beings are created to govern nature and that the sun, moon, and planets are created to assist us in our task of governing. Carey thought that the heavenly bodies ought to be carefully studied since the Creator had made them to be signs or markers. They help divide the monotony of space into directions—East, West, North, and South; and of time into days, years, and seasons. They make it possible for us to devise calendars; study geography and history; to plan our lives, our work, and our social order. The culture of astronomy sets us free to be rulers, whereas the culture of astrology makes us subjects, our lives determined by our stars.

"Introduction of Astronomy was an attempt to introduce western classical education into India: Trivium and Quadrivium. Trivium studied *words* while quadrivium focussed on *numbers*. The latter included study of mathematics, geometry, music and astronomy. Carey's generation believed that God had written two books: The book of His words (the Bible) and the book of His works (in nature and culture). To know Truth required us to study both the books. Language (Trivium) needed to be studied to understand God's word and

Numbers (Quadrivium) needed to be studied to understand the book of God's works in nature."

LIBRARY PIONEER

A postgraduate student of library science stands up next. "William Carey pioneered the idea of lending libraries in the Subcontinent. While the East India Company was importing shiploads of ammunition and soldiers to subdue India, Carey asked his friends in the Baptist Missionary Society to load educational books and seeds into those same ships. He believed that would facilitate his task of regenerating Indian soil and empowering Indian people to embrace ideas that would free their minds. Carey's objective was to create indigenous literature in the vernacular. But until such literature was available, Indians needed to receive knowledge and wisdom from around the world, to catch up quickly with other cultures. He wanted to make such knowledge available to Indians through lending libraries."

FOREST CONSERVATIONIST

"William Carey was an evangelist," begins a student from the Indian Forest Institute. "He thought that, 'If the Gospel flourishes in India, the wilderness will, in every respect, become a fruitful field.' He became the first person in India to write essays on forestry, almost fifty years before the government made its very first attempt at forest conservation, in Malabar. Carey both practiced and vigorously advocated the cultivation of timber, giving practical advice on how to plant trees for environmental, agricultural, and commercial purposes. His motivation came from his belief that God has made man responsible for the earth. It was in response to Carey's journal, *Friend of India*, that the government first appointed Dr. Brandis of Bonn to care for the forests of Burma, and arranged for the supervision of the forests of South India by Dr. Clegham."

CRUSADER FOR WOMEN'S RIGHTS

"William Carey," says a feminist social science scholar, "was the first man to stand against both the ruthless murders and the widespread oppression of women—virtually synonymous with Hinduism in the eighteenth and nineteenth centuries. The male in India was crushing the female through polygamy, female infanticide, child marriage, widow-burning, euthanasia, and forced female illiteracy—all sanctioned by religion. The British government timidly accepted these social evils as being an irreversible and intrinsic part of India's religious mores. Carey began to conduct systematic sociological and scriptural research on these issues. He published his reports in order to raise public opinion and protest both in Bengal and England. He influenced a whole generation of civil servants—his students at Fort William College—to resist these evils. Carey opened schools for girls. When widows converted to Christianity, he arranged marriages for them. It was Carey's persistent, twenty-five-year battle against *sati*, widow-burning, which finally led to Lord Bentinck's famous Edict in 1829, banning one of the most abominable of all religious practices."

PUBLIC SERVANT

"William Carey," says a student of public administration, "initially was not allowed to enter British India because the East India Company was against the proselytising of Hindus. Therefore, Carey worked in the Danish territory of Serampore. But because the Company could not find a suitable professor of Bengali for Fort William College, Carey was later invited to teach there. During his professorship, lasting thirty years, Carey transformed the ethos of the British administration from indifferent imperial exploitation to 'civil' service.

"Everywhere, an officer of the state was a servant of the emperor. He looked after the interests of the Emperor, not the people. That changed when British evangelicals embraced some of the principles that came out of the German Reformation. The Reformers taught that a "civil servant" must be God's servant, commissioned to take care for God's children. German Reformation made a civil servant a "priest" appointed by God to serve the common good. Carey's team injected that biblical principle into Indian Civil Services."

MORAL REFORMER

"William Carey," reflects a student of Indian philosophy, "revived the ancient idea that ethics and morality were inseparable from religion. Traces of this assumption can be seen in *Vedic* worldview. The *Upanishadic* teachers, however, separated ethics from spirituality. They thought that the human self (*Atman*) was the divine Self (*Brahma*). Therefore, our spirit cannot sin; our *Atman* only gets deluded and begins to imagine itself as distinct from God. What we require is not deliverance from sin but enlightenment, that is, a direct experience of our divinity that is free from the dualism of good and evil. This denial of human sinfulness and emphasis on our inherent divinity made it possible for us in India to be intensely 'religious' yet at the same time unabashedly immoral. In fact, an "enlightened" soul was required to do some evil to demonstrate that it had been delivered from commonplace morality.

"Carey began re-affirming the Bible's idea that human beings were sinners and needed both forgiveness for sin and deliverance from its power over them. He taught that it was not ignorance but sin that had separated us from God and that it was impossible to please God without holiness. According to Carey, true spirituality began only when we repented of our sins. This teaching revolutionised the nineteenth-century religious scene in India. For example, after Raja Ram Mohun Roy, one of the greatest Hindu scholars of the nineteenth century, came in contact with Carey and the other missionaries at Serampore, he began to question seriously the spirituality then prevalent in India. He summed up his conclusions thus:

> The consequence of my long and uninterrupted research into religious truth has been that I have found the doctrine of Christ more conducive to moral principles, and better adapted for the use of rational beings, than any other which has come to my knowledge.

CULTURAL TRANSFORMER

A student of history stands up last. "Dr. William Carey is the father of the Indian Renaissance of the nineteenth century that birthed modern India. Hindu India had reached its intellectual, artistic, architectural, and literary zenith by the eleventh century A.D. Once Adi Shankaracharya's idea that everything is one (Monism) began to sweep the Indian subcontinent, the creative springs of humanity dried up, and India's great decline began. The material environment, human rationality, and all that enriches human culture became suspect. Asceticism, untouchability, mysticism, the occult, superstition, idolatry, witchcraft, and other oppressive beliefs and practices became the hallmark of Indian culture. The invasion, exploitation, and resulting political dominance of foreign rulers made matters worse.

"Into this chaos, came Carey and initiated the process of India's reform. He saw India not as a foreign country to be exploited, but as his (heavenly) Father's land to be loved and served, a society where truth, not ignorance, needed to rule. Carey's movement culminated in the birth of the idea of India as a nation and nationalism as an ethical virtue. These became the foundations of India's political unity and independence.

"Carey believed that God's image was in man, not in idols; therefore, it was oppressed humanity—not idols—that ought to be served.

"He thought that we needed to understand and rule over nature instead of fearing, appeasing, or worshiping it. He taught the Bible's idea that to be spiritual means to develop one's intellect instead of killing it, as meditation, Yoga and Tantra had taught. Carey brought printing and universal education to India because he thought that we needed to enjoy literature and culture instead of shunning it as *maya*.

"Carey's this-worldly spirituality, with as strong an emphasis on justice and love for one's fellows, as on love for God, marked the turning point of Indian culture from a downward to an upward trend. The early Indian leaders of the Hindu Renaissance, such as Raja Ram Mohun Roy, Keshub Chandra Sen, and others, drew their inspiration from William Carey and the missionaries associated with him."

So, *who was William Carey?*

William Carey, the pioneer of the modern Christian missionary movement, is the Father of Modern India. While colonialism was subjugating India militarily and commercially, he began liberating the Indian mind which united fragmented Indian states into one nation and culminated in our political independence. Carey was an evangelist who used every available medium to illumine every dark facet of Indian life with the light of truth. As such, he is a central character in the story of India's modernisation.

Chapter Two

WILLIAM CAREY: A TRIBUTE BY AN INDIAN WOMAN

I LOVE VISITING CALCUTTA. Two hundred years after William Carey lived there, women are still treated more respectfully there than in most parts of India.

In Lucknow in North India, where I grew up and went to college, it was usual for a woman to be looked upon as a sex object. All my girlfriends accepted this fate. I too was unable to look upon myself as an individual with inherent dignity. It is liberating to be respected.

Bengal was not always as courteous as it is now. Nor can we take it for granted that India will continue to treat women with civility. As India turns her back on the legacy of her reformers, her decline is predictable. *The Times of India* (New Delhi, May 22, 1993) reported the following about a university campus in North India:

> "Parents are withdrawing their wards from the women's college as lumpen elements have been allowed access to the college premises, which includes girls' hostels, even at night—something unthinkable a couple of years ago. Most faculty members and students keep away from the University activities."

The result is that the once lively campus has been reduced to a fear-stricken place. The only solace for the administration is that the situation in most other universities in the country, particularly in Uttar Pradesh, is no better.

Allahabad was an important matrix of literary and political influence before Independence and gave us five prime ministers in the first four decades of freedom, including India's only woman Prime Minister, Indira Gandhi. Missionaries had transformed it into one of the premier educational centers in North India. Today, girls cannot walk freely on the university campus.

The decline in respect for women in the institutes of learning ought to convince us that education by itself is not enough. It should also give us a glimpse of what a woman's life would have been without the influence of William Carey. A brief review of his achievement in restoring women's God-given dignity and individuality will make it obvious why I choose to honour him.

THE INDIA THAT CAREY SAW

In his classic study, *Modern Religious Movements in India*, J.N. Farquhar writes:

> "When Carey came, Hindus were in a pitifully backward condition. Learning had almost ceased; ordinary education scarcely existed; spiritual religion was to be met only in the quietest places; and a coarse idolatry with cruel and immoral rites held all the great centers of population. Mohammedanism was very orthodox and ignorant, and steadily deteriorating. The collapse of their governments and decline of the Muslim character had worked sad havoc in their religion. There was no living movement of thought and no spiritual leader amongst them."

Needless to say, women, being far behind men in most areas of culture and learning, were the saddest victims of this mental and spiritual deprivation. Sir W. W. Hunter observed in a similar vein:

> "When Carey landed in India, Hinduism was in full vigor—its

customs, traditions, institutions, and laws were all unchanged. The country was practically untouched by any regenerative influence whatsoever. He had to encounter in its worst forms all the strength of the Hindu system."

"WHERE, O DEATH, IS THY STING?"

Carey's love for and dedication to the people of India is beyond dispute; yet he did not romanticise its darkness as so many of us do. The following excerpt from a letter Carey wrote to John Williams in New York expresses his deep grief for India:

> "No people can have more surrendered their reason. In business, they are not deficient, but in religion, they seem without understanding. But a people can hardly be better than their gods. They have made idols after their own hearts. Hindus have not the fierceness of American Indians, but this is abundantly made up for by cunning and deceit. Moral rectitude makes no part of their religious system; no wonder, therefore they are immersed in impurity."

Men may have surrendered their reason, but for women to attempt to develop or use their reasoning powers was considered sacrilegious. Superstitions and moral impurities are not abstract evils. Their practical consequence is to sear human conscience so effectively as to make life hell for the weak.

To another correspondent, Carey wrote that no other land had seen such a lethal combination of "false principles" as India. In other lands, he lamented,

> "Conscience may often be appealed to with effect. Here God's law is erased thence, and an idolatrous ceremony is engraved in its stead. The multitudes pay a thousand-fold more deference to the Brahmins than the people did to the priests in Papacy's darkest days. And all are bound to their present state by caste, in breaking

whose chains a man must endure to be renounced and abhorred by his wife, children, and friends. Every tie that twines around the heart of a husband, father, and neighbour must be torn and broken, here a man can give himself to Christ."

Carey's journal often expresses the heaviness of his heart concerning India's spiritual condition. Here is a typical entry:

"Many [Hindus] say that the Gospel is the word of truth; but they abound so much in flattery and encomiums... that little can be said respecting their sincerity. The very common sins of lying and avarice are so universal also, that no European who has not witnessed it can form an idea of their various appearances: They will stoop to anything whatsoever to get a few cowries, and lie on every occasion."

"THE STING OF DEATH IS SIN."

"Sin enslaves," said Jesus. Many of us forget that slavery is a social reality. While slavery works to the advantage of some, it hurts the weak. In struggling for the emancipation of women, Carey was resisting the consequences of those sins that ruled India in his day.

Obviously, women were not the only ones who suffered slavery. About the rigid caste system, Carey writes:

"Perhaps this is one of the strongest chains with which the devil ever bound the children of men. This is my comfort, that God can break it."

Besides being oppressive, the caste system,

"... cut off all motives to inquiry and exertion, and made stupid contentment the habit of their lives. Their minds resembled their mud homesteads, devoid of pictures, ornaments and books. Harmless, indifferent, vacant, they plod on in the path of their forefathers; and even truths in geography, astronomy, or any other science, if out of their beaten track, make no more impression on them than the sublimer truths of religion."

Carey, of course, did not make this observation about the distinctive condition of women. But women are primarily the homemakers. The absence of pictures and books in their mud homesteads was a reflection of the systematic emptying of the female mind—a mind that God had created to be filled with all that is intellectually true, morally noble, culturally good, and aesthetically beautiful.

"Yet, [writes Carey's biographer S. Pearce Carey] he pitied more than blamed their superstition and servility, [which,] he would often say, came of long subservience, making him the keener to preach to these dull, passive captives. They had been so drilled to regard Brahmins as "sort of half-divinities," that they attributed even the spots on the sun and moon and the sea's saltiness to their [Brahmins'] vexed potent curses."

Kali, the goddess of death, is the patron deity of Calcutta and most other parts of Bengal where Carey came with the good news of a God who died to give us life. Divinity was perceived in Bengal as *Ardhanareeshwara*—half male and half female—and yet women there were held in the lowest possible esteem. As a contemporary journalist, Shakuntala Narasimhan puts it so aptly in her book on *sati*: "[Woman] was deified in the abstract and demeaned in real life."

It has been stated often enough that, "In Hinduism, there is no salvation for a woman until she be reborn a man." Her only hope lies in serving man in complete self-abnegation. Female infanticide, child marriage, *purdah*, dowry, and *sati* were every day realities accepted as normal by the learned pundits and illiterate masses. What was the common thread that linked all these practices together? Obviously an ignorance of the truth that woman shares with man the glory of being in God's own image; and the consequent diabolical trivialisation of woman's God-given dignity. To quote, again, Shakuntala Narasimhan's description of the treatment of women:

"Smothered or poisoned at birth, given away in marriage at a tender age, bargained over like some commodity by dowry-hungry in-laws, secluded in the name of chastity and religion, and finally burned for the exaltation of the family's honour, or shunned as [an] inauspicious widow, the burden of oppression took different stages of a woman's life, from birth to death in a chain of attitudes linked by contempt for the female."

The apostle Paul said that "The sting of death is sin." (1 Corinthians 15:56) The sins of India, such as idolatry and caste, resulted in death in more ways than one. Carey struggled against sin; he struggled to give the knowledge of the truth about God; the truth about" who men

 really are as seen by their Creator, not as defined by the pundits; he struggled for freedom and for life.

Let us first examine some of Carey's struggles against various methods of murdering women, and then turn to his efforts for breaking the yoke of oppression.

"WHERE, O DEATH, IS THY VICTORY?"

Infanticide

The practice of exposing infants to death was a widespread religious custom in Carey's day, and it still exists today. If an infant was sick, it was supposed that he was under the influence of an evil spirit. He was put into a basket and hung up for three days. Only if the child survived were means then used to save his life.

In 1794, near Malda, Carey had his first horrifying experience of infanticide. He found the remains of an infant devoured by white ants after having been offered as a sacrifice. He could never be content after that with the mere telling of the story of a Savior who had died for humanity, including the little ones. Carey felt obligated to struggle to save their lives.

Every winter at the Sagar *mela*, where the sea and the River Hooghly meet, children were pushed down the mud banks into the sea to be either drowned or devoured by crocodiles, all in fulfillment of vows their mothers had made. This was looked upon as a most holy sacrifice—giving to Mother Ganges the fruit of their bodies for the sins of their souls. As Carey's concern for these victims of superstitious beastliness became known, he was asked by the British governor general to inquire into the numbers, nature, and reasons for infanticide. Carey said that he took this assignment with great readiness. His report resulted in the practice being outlawed. The moment of satisfaction came when Carey's group went to the Sagar *puja* (worship of the ocean) in 1804 to proclaim the story of God's own sacrifice. They found that due to administrative vigilance, not a single infant could be sacrificed to the goddess. What a victory: A wicked "religious" practice had been suppressed.

Widowhood and *Widow-Burning*

When the much older husbands died, their widows were subjected to a terrible plight, because they were perceived as bad omens who had brought about the deaths of their husbands. It was believed that a widow had "eaten her husband." The widows who were not victims of *sati* had to live a life of austerity. This belief was a rationalisation. The reality was that a widow was looked upon not as a precious individual in need of support to start a new life but as an economic liability. Her parents had already given the bride price (dowry); the parents-in-law were not willing to part with their "possessions" and return the dowry to get the young widow remarried. And, of course, the illiterate widow was in no position to earn and become an economic asset for the family.

To add insult to injury, the bereaved widow had to shave off her hair, remove all jewelry, and wear white, all to avoid attracting the other men in the family and causing them to go astray. She had to be kept indoors to keep her chaste. Widows were generally not allowed to remarry, but *niyoga* (which is not the same as remarriage) was practiced. It meant that the widow was required to cohabit with her brother-in-law or another male relative, for the purpose of producing a son to offer religious oblations for the deceased husband, if he had no sons of his own to undertake this important religious rite.

The Widow Remarriage Act did not come into effect until 1856, for the first time making it legal for a widow to remarry. Until then the only options for a widow were either to commit *sati* or to suffer lifelong indignity and hardship. *Sati* often seemed the lesser of the two evils, the widows preferring a speedy death to the unknown horrors of widowhood. They were deluded into thinking that by their act of self-sacrifice, they would bestow a celebrity status on the family, and would take seven generations of their family, before and after them, to heaven. They were assured that the heroic act of self-immolation would deify them as *sati-mata* and, supremely, they would be considered "pativrata."

Shuddhitatva describes a *pativrata* woman:

All the actions of a woman should be the same as that of her husband. If her husband is happy, she should be happy, if he is sad, she should be sad, and if he is dead, she should also die. Such a wife is called *pativrata*.

One evening at Naoserai in 1799, Carey witnessed firsthand the cruelty of *sati*. He gave the following moving description in a letter to Andrew Fuller:

"We saw a number of people assembled by the riverside. I asked for what they were met, and they told me, to burn the body of the dead man. I inquired if his wife would die with him; they answered, "Yes" and pointed to her.

She was standing by the pile of large billets of wood, on the top of which lay her husband's dead body. Her nearest relative stood by her; and near her was a basket of sweetmeats. I asked if this was her choice, or if she were brought to it by any improper influence. They answered that it was perfectly voluntary. I talked till reasoning was of no use, and then began to exclaim with all my might against what they were doing, telling them it was shocking murder. They told me it was a great act of holiness, and added in a very surly manner, that if I did not like to see it, I might go further off and desired me to do so. I said that I would not go, that I was determined to stay and see the murder, against which I should certainly bear witness at the tribunal of God.

I exhorted the widow not to throw away her life; to fear nothing, for no evil would follow her refusal to be burned. But in the most calm manner she mounted the pile, and danced on it with her hands extended, as if in the utmost tranquility of spirit. Previous to this, the relative, whose office it was to set fire to the pile, led her five times around it-thrice at a time.

As she went round, she scattered the sweetmeats amongst the people, who ate them as a very holy thing. This being ended, she lay down beside the corpse and put one arm under its neck, and the other over it, when a quantity of dry cocoa leaves and other substances were heaped over them to a considerable height, and then *ghee* was poured on the top. Two bamboos were then put over them and held fast down, and fire was put to the pile, which immediately blazed fiercely, owing to the dry and combustible materials of which it was composed.

No sooner was the fire kindled than all the people set up a great shout of joy; invoking *Siva*. It was impossible to have heard the woman, had she groaned, or even cried aloud, on account of the shoutings of the people, and again it was impossible for her to stir or struggle, by reason of the bamboos held down on her, like the levers of a press.

We made such an objection to their use of these, insisting that it was undue force, to prevent her getting up when the fire burned. But they declared it was only to keep the fire from falling down. We could not bear to see more, and left them, exclaiming loudly against the murder, and filled with horror at what we had seen."

That funeral pyre set Carey's spirit aflame with anguish. His brain burned with her body. His sensitivity and compassion naturally extended over to the children who had lost their father. In their mother, they would have had, at least, a natural guardian, their tenderest and most faithful and watchful friend. But her cruel death left them orphaned in one sad day.

The culture that glorified this cruelty had clearly put family possessions above the intrinsic value of a woman's life. Carey vowed, (as did Abraham Lincoln in America later concerning the auction of slave women) "to hit this accursed thing hard if God should spare him."

The weavers (*Kories*) buried their dead, so their widows had to be buried alive. Carey describes how a pit was dug and the widow sat in it with the body of her dead husband in her lap. The family then threw in mud,

> ... and after a short space, two of them descend into the grave and tread the earth firmly around the body of the widow. She sees the earth rising higher and higher around her without upbraiding her murderers, or making the least effort to arise and make her escape. At length, the earth reaches the head of the suffocating widow— the mother.

THE ABOLITION OF *SATI*

In 1802 Lord Wellesley asked William Carey to institute an enquiry into *sati*. Carey sent out people who investigated carefully the cases of *sati* within a thirty-mile radius of Calcutta, and they discovered the "damning" total of 438 widow burnings, "... the toll of a single year's superstition, cruelty, and waste."

Armed with these facts, Carey implored the government to ban *sati*. Tragically for the Indian widows, Lord Wellesley had to leave India before he could take action, and his successors were unwilling to interfere with the religious sentiments of the people. The legal prohibition of *sati* was stalled for yet another quarter of a century.

Carey knew that Hindu polytheism is false in teaching that the husband is *patidev*—a woman's god. Marriage does not exhaust the totality of what a woman is. Therefore, Carey fought against the idea that a woman's life ceases to be valuable after her husband's death. We can be grateful that Carey did not see himself merely as a servant, but also as a fighter. Service, without fighting, can often mean only the strengthening of the social status quo.

For Carey, "fighting" did not merely mean "agitating," as it so often means today. It also meant educating. So Carey researched and wrote. It was his article in his newspaper, *Friend of India*, that became the central document for debate on *sati* in, and outside the British Parliament.

Carey considered this battle against a social evil as a spiritual battle against religious darkness and the forces of death. He prayed and got others to pray. One of his prominent prayer partners in this matter was William Wilberforce, an evangelical member of Parliament in England and the leader of the movement for the abolition of Britain's slave trade. Wilberforce struggled in prayer both for the emancipation of the African slaves and for the plight of Indian women.

Carey's great day came when, on December 4, 1829, Lord Cavendish Bentinck, after one year of careful study, declared *sati* both illegal and criminal, by Regulation XVII of the Bengal Code. The Edict was sent to Carey for translation on Sunday, December 6. Carey jumped with joy, and abandoned his plan to preach on that Sunday, in order to carry out the "fast unto the Lord," spoken of in Isaiah 58:6 . At long last widows were legally free to live as human beings, and no longer would children be cruelly orphaned in the name of "religion."

BREAKING THE YOKES OF OPPRESSION

Child Marriage

Initially, a sexually promiscuous society sounds free, but eventually, it must curtail a woman's liberty in order to protect her. The advocates of compulsory education have discovered that parents will not send their daughters to school if it means sending them as far as the next village. It is dangerous since neither the men nor the girls themselves can be trusted. To guard her safety, and to uphold her family's honour, getting her married off at the earliest age possible is the best safeguard. Childhood is thus denied to a girl. She has to pass into motherhood before she has time to grow as a person.

The last census of the nineteenth century in Bengal revealed that, in and around Calcutta alone, there were ten thousand widows under the age of four and more than fifty thousand between the ages of five and nine. All these child widows were victims of child marriage.

Polygamy was also a common practice in Carey's day. Sometimes fifty women were given to one Brahmin man so that their families could boast that they were allied by marriage to a *Kulin* (high caste). Even Ram Mohun Roy, who later supported many of Carey's reforms, was married three times by his father when he was a child. His first wife died at a very early age. Then, when he was about nine years old, his father married him to two different wives within an interval of less than twelve months.

Child marriage was outlawed only in 1929 when the Child Marriages Restraint Act was introduced. However, this, as we all know, is only "legislation on paper." Even cabinet ministers in some Indian states get their children married off at a tender age. No social problem, if it is rooted in the moral/religious soil of a culture, can be easily eradicated legally. Carey understood this and did not agitate against child marriage as such. Instead, he sought to undercut its moral roots through the teaching of the Bible, and its social roots through female education.

But the practice of child marriage tended to preclude the possibility of educating Indian women. This, in turn, deprived them of intellectual and cultural development. They became dependent and vulnerable to oppression, exploitation, and enslavement. In seeking to educate girls, Carey was also undermining their dependency, a chief source of their slavery.

Female Education

The following statement of a Hindu father to a missionary about the education of his children is a typical example of the traditional Indian attitude Carey had to confront:

> "You may educate my sons, and open to them all the stores of knowledge: But my daughters you must not approach, however, benevolent your designs. Their ignorance and seclusion are essentially necessary to the honour of my family; a consideration of far greater moments with me than any mental cultivation of which I cannot estimate the benefit. They must be married at an age when your plans of education could scarcely commence."

Hannah Marshman took on the education problem. She was a decided asset to Carey's community in Serampore. A warm, pious, and prudent woman, she not only ran the household but also started a boarding school for the children of missionaries and other Europeans. This was an exemplary contrast to what Indian housewives were allowed to do with their lives and talents. This venture also greatly helped defray the expenses of the mission. By the end of the first year, in

1801, the boarding school showed a profit of Rs. 300. With this success Mrs. Marshman was able to start schools for Indian boys and girls.

The success resulted in the establishment of the Calcutta Baptist Female School Society in 1819, and an additional school for girls in Calcutta. During 1820–30, Carey's mission in Serampore took the lead in bringing about the beginning of the revolution of modern education for the women of rural Bengal, which led in turn to the founding of other girls' schools in Benares, Dacca, and Allahabad.

The immediate impact of these schools was apparent to all observers. Mrs. Ann Judson, for example, wrote in a letter to her sister about the Mission Charity School near Dr. Carey's house:

> ... with two-hundred boys and nearly as many girls—chiefly children picked up from the streets, of no caste. We could see them kneel in prayer together, and hear them sing. It was most affecting.

Free schools for the low castes and the outcasts were always a chief feature of Carey's work, and these were started within a twenty-mile radius of Serampore, where almost 8,000 children attended.

Carey did not limit himself to giving only primary education to women. The Serampore College was launched in order to offer higher education in the vernacular. The Serampore Mission Girl's High School began in 1827 and became an inspiration for Savitri Bai Phule's school which was founded in 1848.

In 1827, Hannah's husband, Dr. Joshua Marshman also obtained for Serampore a charter to confer degrees in all faculties, making it the first college in India to do so. Until today, the Serampore Senate remains the only university in India to confer degrees in divinity.

These women missionaries pioneered education for women in India. Without their heroic and sacrificial efforts the potential of women in India would still be untapped.

I got a feel for the price these women paid when I came back to India from the United States, married Vishal, and in 1976, driven by my

God-given love for India, went to live in rural Madhya Pradesh for the first eight years of my married life. The toilet was outdoors; drinking water had to come from three kilometers away; the nearest medical facilities were thirteen kilometers away; and if we wanted to buy bread and butter, we had to travel more than 200 kilometers to Jhansi—a tortuous six-hour journey during and after the monsoons!

Both our daughters were born there. Rural life is not "romantic" when you have to spend much of your energy protecting your children, not merely from flies and mosquitoes, but also from snakes and scorpions falling from your thatched roof. I found it a daunting challenge to expose my daughters to the dangers of contagious diseases such as TB and leprosy in order to serve women who were not always cooperative, let alone able to understand me.

What would you do when a fifteen-year-old girl, whom you have struggled to help intellectually and culturally, is made pregnant by her stepfather and is quickly married off to prevent his sin from being exposed? Incidents such as these drove me to a sense of hopelessness: Would my sacrifice, hard work, and investment in a precious person amount to anything worthwhile in a climate as decadent as this? The blame cannot be put entirely on men. As I made many friends among the rural women I began to admire them. One of their strengths is their stubbornness. It allows them to smile through life in spite of their social deprivation, domestic oppression, and natural hardships such as crop failures, famines, and floods. But stubbornness also means resistance to change even when they know it to be to their advantage. Stubbornness is the true custodian of the "traditional" India.

Living and serving in rural India for years eventually drove William Carey's wife, Dorothy, insane—and I am not surprised. She was dramatically different from Hannah Marshman and her husband. She had not initially consented to accompany her husband to India, but was talked into changing her mind by Carey's friend, the doctor John

Thomas, and had to board the ship within twenty-four hours—too short a time to pack, let alone prepare herself for the hardships ahead. The ramifications of staying behind with four little children had been an alarming alternative.

Devastating circumstances had overwhelmed Dorothy from the outset. She didn't share her husband's vision. And his many accomplishments in missions, linguistics, printing, journalism, and social reform overshadowed her own struggles with poverty, child-rearing, the heat, mosquitoes, chronic dysentery, and the frequent upheavals as they moved from place to place. All that William Carey was able to accomplish was possible only if he could leave the domestic responsibilities to his wife. But she paid a high price.

For Dorothy's sake, I would have been glad had Carey returned to England. For India's sake, I am grateful that he did not, for the Indian religious culture at that time was completely incapable of producing such a sacrificial missionary spirit. Even now Hindu orthodoxy gives the impression of being much better at producing militant murderers—those who would revive *sati* if they could—than at motivating missionaries who could improve the condition of oppressed women. Women, particularly in rural India, need not only state-sponsored development projects but also women missionaries such as Hannah Marshman.

But our cultural insensitivity has resulted in a policy that refuses visas to missionaries who could improve the status of women. One of the most inhuman results of this policy is in the area of nursing care for the poor. The affluent in India can buy quality care. The poor have to accept constant humiliation in most of our hospitals. Indian culture, even today, does not honour those who serve. Most women who join the nursing profession do so out of economic necessity, not because of a sense of calling. Their cultural conditioning makes them see service as a humiliation and not a high privilege, and they resent their profession and treat their patients harshly as a result.

FOUNDATIONS FOR TRUE FREEDOM

The plight of the Indian woman (or, for that matter, the predicament of an untouchable man) was rooted in a lack of understanding of what a human being is—whether male or female. Secular education, by itself, cannot offer a high view of human life, any more than Hinduism can, for the Indian mindset (formed by notions of reincarnation) makes us no more valuable than animals.

Raja Ram Mohun Roy, Carey's younger contemporary who reinforced many of Carey's reforms, put his finger on the basic problem when he said, "The root of the whole wretched state of the Hindu society was idolatry and the obnoxious superstitions necessarily attached to it."

The later chapters in this book discuss how idolatry lowers a human being's dignity and darkens the mind. Carey lamented about India, "Many perish with cold, many for lack of bread, and millions for lack of knowledge."

He knew that, as his dear window plants were "meant for the sunlight," so was woman-kind made for God. Women could not grow into a true knowledge of themselves, nor enter true liberty which enabled wholesome family and social life, unless they grew in their knowledge of God. Carey strove to make the knowledge of the Savior available to the Indian people.

When he was still on the ship to India, Carey overheard some fishermen tell his companion, Thomas, that they were poor and, therefore, had not read the *Shastras* (the scriptures). Only those who were rich, they said, could read. This implied that spiritual enlightenment and education were reserved for those who had earned enough merit in a previous birth to be born rich or high caste or both. Women, for instance, needed to serve their men well in order to be reborn, hopefully, as men, and to be able, then, to search for salvation. It was partly this fisherman's insight that confirmed in Carey's mind the urgent need to translate, publish, and distribute the Bible, to make the Good News of salvation available to the poor and downtrodden— including the women of India.

This former shoemaker, William Carey, who was no academic, received the gift of "tongues" from the Holy Spirit, to proclaim the Good News to many nationalities. With goal-oriented plodding, he learned many languages. With the help of many pundits, he translated the Bible from the original Hebrew and Greek. He had no dictionaries or grammars to aid him. It was his Bible that informed us that women share with men the glory of being created in God's own image.

The results of making the Bible available were long-term—a true foundation for the work of transformation and salvation. In due time the teaching of the Bible undercut the religious foundations of infanticide, child marriage, *sati*, the burning and burying of lepers, and other forms of human sacrifice. By providing the theological foundations for a belief in the sacredness of human life—both male and female—and by demonstrating that the emancipation of India's women was possible, Carey made certain that his efforts would bless future generations as well as his own.

INDIAN CHRISTIAN WOMEN

William Carey knew that Indian women required ministry from their own "kind"—woman to woman. Only other women could take the knowledge of the truth to the women in *purdah*. What a joy it must have been for Carey when Jaymani became the first Bengali woman to be baptised, in January 1801. The reforming power of the Gospel could now flow to the coming generations with their mother's milk. Even Carey could not have foreseen that Jaymani's conversion was like the small cloud—"as small as a man's hand"—that Elijah saw after three years of famine in Israel. That cloud would soon cover the whole land

and pour down showers of God's blessings. Within a century of Jaymani's conversion, Indian Christian women were to cover the Indian subcontinent. And mass education and universal nursing care followed in its wake. The following observation about the role of Indian Christian women (quoted by J. N. Farquhar in his classic, *The Crown of Hinduism*) was made by a Hindu in 1903:

> "Though cut off from the parent community by religion and by prejudice and intolerance, the Indian Christian woman has been the evangelist of education to hundreds and thousands of Hindu homes. Simple, neat, and kindly, she has won her way to the recesses of orthodoxy, overcoming a strength and bitterness of prejudice of which few outsiders can have an adequate conception. As these sentences are being written, there rises before the mind's eye the picture of scores of tidy, gentle girls, trudging hot and dusty streets barefooted, under a scorching sun, to carry the light of knowledge to homes where they will not be admitted beyond the ante-chamber, and where they cannot get a glass of water without humiliation, yet never complaining, ever patient. To these brave and devoted women wherever they are, friends of female education all over the country will heartily wish "God-speed"."

One hundred years ago, nursing care was almost impossible to obtain in India, except through Indian Christian women. Today, the blessing of nursing care has overflowed from India across the seas to the Muslim nations of the Middle East where nursing care had been unknown. Tens of thousands of Indian Christian nurses are serving the sick in the Gulf States. Often they are humiliated and sexually harassed by people who think that these women are willing to serve men (who are not their husbands) because they are sexually permissive. The fact is that it is the permissiveness of our traditional cultures that had enslaved women.

The Gulf States, as well as India today, can buy services such as education and nursing care, but these societies have yet to realise fully that hygiene, cleanliness, efficiency, honesty, and the overall output of a country are substantially dependent on the position given to women in that society. The irony is that today too many people in the West also need reminding that the salvation of women depends on conversion and moral transformation, not on the worship of goddesses. Mr. Surendranath Bannerjea, noted nationalist and editor of the *Bengalee*, wrote the following in 1911:

> "We have worshipped the goddess of *Sakti* [i.e., energy] for centuries; how is it that through those very centuries we have remained so weak and helpless as a nation? We are the devout worshippers of *Sarasvati* [the goddess of learning]; and at the same time have received a scant share of her blessings. The priests who are the monopolists of the religious rites and ministrations are for the most part as innocent of Vedic knowledge at the present day as the *Sudra* [the Untouchable] was in the days when the gates of knowledge were shut against him by the iron rules of caste. We offer our devotions to *Lakshmi* [the goddess of wealth] every recurrent year; and we remain none the less a nation of paupers."

The orthodox Hindu makes a fetish of certain rules of hygiene formulated by his ancestors in the dim past; he regards it as sin, for instance, to take his meals without bathing; or to remain in unwashed clothes for more than a day; but, with all his religious devotion to the traditional rules of cleanliness, he betrays a strange indifference to the principles of sanitation evolved by modern science, though plague and cholera and all the other diseases that are generated by filth are decimating thousands of his fellow men year after year.

The Hindu father blesses his son's wife with the invocation, "May she be like *Sabitri*." But was there room in ancient Hindu life for the Philistinism which actuates the modern Hindu father to huckster and chaffer over the price of his son with the unfortunate person in search of a bridegroom for his daughter?

It is tragic that a basic lesson that had been learned more than a century ago by enlightened Indians is now being forgotten. That lesson is that the hygiene, health, and wealth of a nation are determined by the position given to women—and not by projects sanctioned by the World Bank, UNESCO, or the World Health Organisation. The status of women is directly proportional to the level of moral purity in a society. And that is what conversion is all about. No wonder Carey was excited by Jaymani's conversion.

CONCLUSION: A SUFFERING SERVANT

William Carey's service was neither smooth nor easy. Struggle marked his life from beginning to end. The difficulties ranged from lack of food and funds to the suffering in his own family and opposition—even from his own mission board in England. His group at Serampore often had to earn their own livelihood as well as raise funds for their own projects. These difficulties would have discouraged anyone who seeks to serve in his own strength. This cobbler, who would have been an untouchable if he had been born in India, plodded on with a goal and a purpose. The fact that he knew that God had commissioned him was one secret of his missionary dynamism. The other source of his sustaining vision was the knowledge that the Gospel was the only power that could liberate India. The Lord who sacrificed His own life to save sinners was both the inspiration and the supreme source of Carey's strength.

Chapter Three

❦

WILLIAM CAREY: A JAR OF CLAY

WAS WILLIAM CAREY A SUPERMAN? A model beyond our reach? Not at all. He, like St. Paul, was conscious that "we have this treasure in jars of clay." The famous passage from 2 Corinthians 4:1–17 was very much the story of Carey's life: "*We are hard pressed on every side, but not crushed; perplexed, but not in despair; persecuted, but not abandoned; struck down, but not destroyed... For our light and momentary troubles are achieving for us an eternal glory that far outweighs them all.*"

If you light a lamp and put it into a jar of clay, you notice that it is through the cracks that the light shines. The solid parts of the jar prevent the light from radiating. It is often the "cracked pots" that God chooses to use. William Carey was one such.

Carey's decision to serve in India cost Dorothy Carey her sanity and her life. In the light of that, how can a woman write a tribute to him? Dorothy's tragedy is indeed the darkest spot in Carey's life. He was human too.

DOROTHY CAREY'S SACRIFICE

Dorothy Plackett Carey was twenty-five and William almost twenty when they married. She resisted going to India—in hindsight with good reason—but went nonetheless. Once there, with seven small children and recurrent bouts of illness, she suffered immensely and eventually went insane. Dorothy Carey unknowingly made a real sacrifice for the Gospel. Her illness was seen as a blot and an embarrassment on Carey's career. Even today mental illness is not something you talk about—even though it is still common in missions.

Biographers have dismissed Dorothy—William Carey's first wife of twenty-six years—in a few sentences. George Smith in his biography *The Life of William Carey* writes:

> "She never learned to share his aspirations or to understand his ideals. Not only did she remain to the last a peasant woman, with a reproachful tongue, but the early hardships of Calcutta and a fever and dysentery clouded the last twelve years of her life with madness.
>
> Almost from the first day of his early married life he had never known the delight of daily converse with a wife able to enter into his scholarly pursuits, and ever to stimulate him in his heavenly quest."

Another writer called Dorothy Carey a "dull commonplace woman" who was "deplorably unsuited to be William's wife."

Charlotte Yonge said of her that "she was a dull, ignorant woman, with no feeling for her husband's high aims or superior powers." These are cruel words. James Beck writes in his book, *Dorothy Carey*:

> Meanwhile, many of these same authors have subjected William to a similar but opposite disservice: overpraise. Sometimes we cannot tell which does us more harm: harsh criticism or bloated praise.

An example of such "overpraise" is this sweeping statement by John Marshman:

> "The extreme consideration and tenderness which invariably marked his conduct towards her, place the meekness and

magnanimity of his character in the strongest light. No word of complaint escaped him."

But Carey did complain. In his journal, he writes, at the beginning of Dorothy's emotional retreat from reality, "I don't love to be always complaining. Yet I always complain." So to suggest that Dorothy's problems never bothered Carey, that he never uttered a word of complaint, or that he never lost patience with her is to place him in an untenable position. He was as human as she. We can, as Beck says, honour and remember him well without having to make ourselves believe he was perfect in all that he ever said or did.

It is true that, instead of signing the register at her wedding, Dorothy put a sign—because she did not know how to read or write. This was not due to a lack of intelligence; there simply was no village school where she grew up. She did later learn to read and write.

They were married for twelve years before William heard the call of God to be a missionary. They had already had six of their seven children when Carey set his heart on his mission—a very risky venture at that time. Dorothy had been adamant about not going with him. No amount of arguments or reasoning seemed to change her mind. Possibly intuition told her that "it would be a sentence of banishment for her and the children," without being able to articulate her reason. Carey's own father had thought him "mad" to go. Some of the factors she must have considered were that she was six months pregnant, already had three little sons, had probably just recovered from her nausea, and the thought of still more nausea—five months of seasickness—would have been enough for her not even to consider the journey. She had heard enough from Carey himself about the tough living conditions and the ravages of tropical disease. It would be hard to imagine, with William so absorbed and interested in sea voyages, that she would not have heard of the scurvy and the many deaths at sea. She probably hated the thought of having to be separated from her close-knit family, the familiar food, and the climate. She probably also knew that going to India as a missionary was illegal.

I agree with Beck that, "Dorothy's decision to stay was a sane and sensible choice rather than an insane and sinful one."

After waiting for six weeks in the south of England and then being asked to leave the ship and told to wait for the Danish ship, Carey, eight-year-old Felix, and Dr. John Thomas showed up one day for breakfast with Dorothy, in a last-ditch effort to get her to change her mind. She remained adamant. Dr. Thomas says he used fear to put pressure on her, saying that if she did not come with them she might never see her husband again. That, it seems, did it, and Dorothy relented, agreeing to accompany them to India, so long as her sister Kitty could go with her.

One can imagine how she felt, having just a few hours in which to pack, sort out her house, and say goodbye to her family, knowing that she might never see them again if she were to succumb, as was likely, to sickness. Meanwhile, the men had to tell the appropriate committee at the Baptist Missionary Society about the change in plans and make the arrangements for the money needed for their tickets.

The Careys and their companions landed in Calcutta after a voyage of five months, in November 1793. It was cooler than normal. There was no one to welcome them or offer them hospitality; they were entering illegally. They were on their own.

Carey at once was preoccupied with putting into practice the Bengali he had learnt on the ship from Dr. Thomas and from preaching to the Bengalis. This was, after all, his passion and his life's goal.

Meanwhile Dorothy, with three boys and a baby, did not know the language and had to look after the children in this strange land with strange food and people who were always staring at her. It seems that Carey did not have much time for the family. Dorothy, with her sister, was largely left alone to care for and feed the family. Kitty was a great support, as was the Thomas family, but they were something of a mixed blessing; financial mistakes resulted in their being hounded by creditors.

Limited funds meant the families were housed poorly, in three separate dwellings in different parts of Calcutta. This in itself was unsettling. After five months, they were offered free land to develop in a tiger-haunted, malaria-infested jungle in south Bengal. It would have meant living in a hut—but an Englishman in a government house came to their rescue. The extreme heat and humidity along with many snakes kept Dorothy in constant fear for her children. She struggled with chronic and debilitating dysentery. Her one support, Kitty, then decided to marry Charles Short, the man who had offered them his house. Dorothy now felt truly alone.

But their conditions were to change for the better. William was offered a manager's job in an indigo factory, with a good salary and a secure house with servants. Very important too was the support of the Udnys—a godly family. But by this time Dorothy must have had enough, and in 1795 she took a turn for the worse. The last straw seems to have been the death of their five-year-old son, Peter. Carey, who was himself very sick, could not find a gravedigger, pallbearer, or casket maker for their son. Isolated from other Christians or Europeans, Carey had to turn to the local Muslims to help him bury Peter—which was taboo for them. The domestic staff refused to touch even the poles of the coffin; to do so would have meant excommunication. This was a very traumatic time for Carey, and it seems for the first time he resorted to an uncustomary outburst of anger at those who threatened to ostracise the only people to whom he could turn for help.

With difficulty, he got four Muslims to dig the grave—with inevitable results. The local community excommunicated the four who then came and complained to Carey. Carey was now faced with a dilemma: Should he stand with these men who had stood with him in his time of need? If he failed to do so, he could expect no help in the future. Gentle persuasion was not going to deliver reconciliation. Instead, Carey angrily sent two men to bring the Muslim leader to his house, by force if necessary and kept him under virtual house arrest while a judge was fetched to settle the matter. The leader was made to eat with the excommunicants—or go hungry. Local traditions had pushed Carey to the limits of his own nature.

For Dorothy, grief at losing her child tipped her over the edge of sanity. She started losing touch with reality. She began to have delusions of Carey's infidelity and would follow him around to catch him red-handed. She would follow him to the factory and publicly accuse him in foul language, shouting obscenities, and causing great embarrassment. She saw Carey as her enemy and sought to get rid of him, even taking a kitchen knife to him. She had to be confined to her room for her own safety and his for twelve years until she died in 1807.

This was enough reason for Carey's biographers to dismiss her. Yet it had been Dorothy's sacrifice that had enabled Carey to do all that he did:

- had she refused to come to India, Carey would have been forced to return to England;
- had she come from an educated upper-class background, she might have completely refused the poor lifestyle they had to accept during the early years, when mission support was not there;
- had she insisted on studying and ministering, they could not have looked after their children in the early years;
- as a result of her mental illness, mission societies began to treat wives as being equally important as their husbands: They were interviewed; their vision, abilities, and mental health were examined, and their needs and concerns were provided for.
- Beck says that Dorothy became the hard anvil on which was hammered some of the success of Carey's remarkable career.

A BEAUTIFUL MARRIAGE

As human beings made in the image of a Triune God, we are made for fellowship and intimacy. Although Carey's decision to marry a Danish countess just a few weeks after Dorothy's death in 1807 was greeted with some dismay, the thirteen years that followed were Carey's most happy and productive. The community realised soon enough that for twelve years Carey had had a marriage in name only. Still, there was some concern that his new wife's physical disabilities—she had been disabled by a fire in early childhood—might be as much a liability for Carey and the community as the mental disabilities they had had to deal with in Dorothy.

Dorothy had been confined for twelve years, two rooms away from Carey's study where he spent long hours. He would have heard her reproaches, her ranting and raving, and yet he had to carry on. Life without a soulmate would have made him very lonely. Yet he was able to accomplish all that he did and manage his children. The wives in their little community stood in as mother to the four boys.

It was only natural that Carey should remarry six months after being widowed. Charlotte Rumohr was a student of Carey's, learning English from him and also learning his faith. Hers had probably been a lifeless Christian faith, but what she saw of this community's faith inspired her, and she went on to take baptism from Carey. She lived next door to the Serampore community and was therefore in close touch with them despite her disabilities; even though she could not walk or talk properly, she had a cheerful spirit. Charlotte was well-read, refined, and had come to India of her own choice. So it was easy for her to love and understand Carey, who by now had probably realised that he had not spent enough time with Dorothy and the children. He was able to be a better husband to Charlotte. Charlotte was deeply interested in him and his work and was a real partner to him spiritually, linguistically, and in his mission; she was particularly concerned about the education of Indian girls.

After Charlotte's death, Carey wrote, "She had lived only for me. Her solicitude for my happiness was incessant and so certainly would she at all time interpret my looks, that any attempt to conceal anxiety or distress of mind would have been in vain."

The following letter to Carey gives us a good feel of the tenderness of their relationship:

> My dearest love—I felt very much in parting with thee, and feel much in being so far from thee .... I am sure thou will be happy and thankful on account of my voice, which is daily getting better, and thy pleasure greatly adds to mine own.
>
> I hope you will not think I am writing too often; I rather trust you will be glad to hear of me .... The good state of my health, the freshness of the air, and the variety of objects enliven my spirits, yet I cannot help longing for you. Pray, my love, take care of your health that I may have the joy to find you well.
>
> I thank thee most affectionately, my dearest love, for thy kind letter. Though the journey is very useful to me, I cannot help feeling much to be so distant from you, but I am much with you in my thoughts.... The Lord be blessed for the kind protection He has given to His cause in a time of need. May He still protect and guide and bless His dear cause, and give us all hearts growing in love and zeal.... I felt very much affected in parting with thee. I see plainly it would not do to go from you; my heart cleaves to you. I need not say (for I hope you know my heart is not insensible) how much I feel your kindness in not minding any expense for the recovery of my health. You will rejoice to hear me talk in my old way, and not in that whispering manner. I feel so much pleasure in writing to you, my love, that I cannot help doing it. I was nearly disconcerted by Mrs. __ laughing at my writing so often; but then, I thought, I feel

so much pleasure in receiving your letters that I may hope you do the same.

I thank thee, my love, for thy kind letter.

One cannot help but feel glad for Carey that after twenty-six years he had found fulfillment in his domestic life. His financial and domestic problems were now behind him. In 1813, the Parliament had given permission for missionaries to go to India. Some young men did come to help the veteran missionaries. But they soon became headaches for the old guards. Carey went through the conflicts with colleagues we all go through. One factor that sustained him through those years was the fact that there was now one person who loved him, believed in him, cared for him, and sustained him.

CREATIVE LEISURE

William Carey was an unusually well-rounded man. When he worked with his hands as a shoemaker, he cultivated his mind. Learning was a hobby. Later, when he worked with his mind as a translator, he relaxed with his hands—in gardening and forestry. Even as a child growing up in England in poverty, Drewery says, Carey

> "... displayed a passionate interest in his surroundings, particularly in plants and animals. If he had set his heart on obtaining any particular flower or insect for his collection, he was heedless of dirt or discomfort in the pursuit of it. His bedroom was filled with specimens, with birds and insects both alive and dead, which would indicate that his mother must have shown commendable tolerance of her son's enthusiasm."

Carey had been primarily a cordwainer—a little more skilled than a shoemaker. His father Edmund was a weaver, later a schoolmaster and parish clerk. Even though the Careys were very poor, William's father planted in him the seeds of learning. Edmund had a special interest in the education of women, at a time when it was not considered important for women to be literate. He was a man of initiative and a model for William.

Carey had to stop his formal studies at twelve years of age to earn a living. He tried his hand as an agricultural labourer, but his sensitive skin prevented him from being in the sun too long. Northampton was then an important place for shoemaking, so the obvious thing was to learn an indoor job. Carey joined Clarke Nichols as an apprentice. There his fellow apprentice John Warr was to take this sixteen-year-old boy to a meeting of Dissenters, where he was converted.

It seems that as a shoemaker Carey kept both his hands and his mind active. It was probably there while making shoes that he thought up his sermons, and looked at his huge world map on which he had put information gleaned from his reading of Captain James Cook's voyages. He also made a large leather map with all the countries of the world on it. His friends nicknamed him Columbus because of his fascination with sea voyages.

Carey's thirst for knowledge was insatiable and led him to learn Greek on his own, just by asking another student for help and going through Mr. Nichols's library. He was to learn Hebrew and Latin too, on his own initiative. He also had miles and miles to walk to sell his shoes—times when his mind was busy preparing sermons.

In England, wherever he lived, Carey managed to have a garden around his cottage. In India he continued with his botanical interests, putting his heart and soul into getting and growing plants. He had a huge, beautiful garden of which he was justly proud. He writes to a friend that he is,

> "passionately fond of nature and that I relax my mind from pursuits of a more labourious kind by attending thereto. My museum and garden are therefore not only sources of pleasure but of health to me."

Carey's five-acre arboretum in Serampore had trees such as eucalyptus, mahogany, deodar, teak, and tamarind. These trees were unknown in Calcutta. By June 1800, just six months after arriving in Serampore, he was to tell his friend William Roxburgh of the 427 species of plants he had in his garden.

Carey's youngest son Jonathan writes about his father's powers of observation and his natural curiosity for all of God's creation:

"In objects of nature, my father was exceedingly curious. His collection of mineral ores, and other objects of natural history, was extensive and obtained his particular attention in seasons of leisure and recreation. The science of botany was his constant delight and study; and his fondness for his garden remained to the last. No one was allowed to interfere in the arrangements of this his favorite retreat; and it is here he enjoyed his most pleasant moments of secret devotion and meditation. The arrangements made by him were on the Linnaean system; and to disturb the bed or border of his garden was to touch the apple of his eye. He had the best and rarest botanical collection of plants in the East, to the extension of which, by his correspondence with persons of eminence in Europe and other parts of the world his attention was constantly directed and in return he supplied his correspondents with rare collections from the East. It was painful to observe with what distress my father quitted this scene of his enjoyments, when extreme weakness, during his last illness, prevented his going to his favorite retreat. Often when he was unable to walk, he was drawn into the garden in a chair placed on a board with four wheels."

Carey's passion in obtaining botanic samples is revealed in his request to his son Jabez, who was going as a missionary to Amboina. He says:

"Be sure to send me every possible vegetable production. Plant tubers and bulbs in a box so thickly as to touch one another, or hang them dry in a well-covered basket in an airy part of the ship.

Send, if you can, two or three hundred of each sort. I shall be glad of the smallest as well as the largest common plants. Think none insignificant. Plant the small in boxes, and always keep some well-rooted and ready; if too recently planted, they die on the way. Just before dispatching them sow very thickly amongst them seeds of trees, fruits and shrubs, covered with a finger's thickness of fresh soil. They should be watered a little on the voyage. You must often send the same thing, as it will be ten to one that they arrive alive. So send abundant seeds of every sort, perfectly ripe and dry, in named paper packets, in a box or basket, secured from the rats; and, if possible, cite the due soil. Parasitical plants, such as you have seen me tie on trees, need only be stripped where they grow, and hung in baskets in an airy part of the ship, or even at the maintop. All boxes of plants must have strips of wood over them, to keep out the rats. Nothing must be put in the hold. Send me as many live birds as possible; also small quadrupeds, monkeys etc. Beetles, lizards, frogs, serpents may be put in a small keg of rum. I have much confidence in you to add greatly to my stock of natural productions. But you must persevere in both collecting and sending."

Just reading these instructions is exhausting, and yet this was Carey's leisure-time pursuit. He was not only a translator, a teacher, and a reformer but also a serious botanist.

He edited three volumes of his friend William Roxburgh's *Flora Indica*, which is still a standard work with botanists. On the title page of this major publication he wrote, "All thy works praise thee, O Lord—David."

In 1823, Carey was elected a fellow of the Linnaean Society of London. He also became a member of the Geological Society of London and a corresponding member of the Horticultural Society of London.

BEAUTY OUT OF ASHES

Carey was in Calcutta when Marshman broke the news to him—just when the printing and translation work was at its height—that a devastating fire had ravaged the hall that housed their printing press.

During the day this hall, which was 200 feet long and 50 feet wide, had housed at least twenty *munshis* working on different translations, along with the type-founders, compositors, pressmen, binders, and writers.

This huge fire had consumed Carey's manuscripts along with ten Bible translations. His translation of the epic *Ramayana*, which he had translated along with Marshman, was also gone. His huge project of the polyglot Sanskrit dictionary—his *magnum opus*—was now just ashes. Vast quantities of English paper, fourteen fonts of Oriental types, new supplies of Hebrew, Greek, and English type, priceless dictionaries, grammars, steel punches, deeds, and account books of the property were all gone.

As Carey returned and surveyed the scene with the chaplain of Fort William, he said, with tears in his eyes,

> "In one short evening the labours of years are consumed. How unsearchable are the ways of God. I had lately brought some things to the utmost perfection of which they seemed capable, and contemplated the missionary establishment with perhaps too much self-congratulation. The Lord has laid me low, that I may look more simply to him."

Thomason, an eyewitness, writes:

> "Who could stand in such a place, at such a time with such a man, without feelings of sharp regret and solemn exercise of mind? I saw the ground strewed with half-consumed paper, on which in the course of a very few months the words of life would have been printed. The misshapen lumps-the sad remains of beautiful types

consecrated to the service of the sanctuary. All was smiling and promising a few hours before-now all is vanished into smoke or converted into rubbish. Return now to thy books, regard God in all thou doest. Let God be exalted in all thy plans and purposes and labours. He can do without thee."

Earlier Carey had been comforted by a colleague at Fort William College. "However vexing it may be, a road the second time traveled is usually taken with more confidence and ease than at the first."

This is exactly what Carey braced himself to do. He decided that the "Phoenix arising anew from the ashes" might be a myth, but "we have indeed been promised a crown of beauty, instead of ashes":

> "The Spirit of the Sovereign Lord is on me, because the Lord has anointed me to preach good news to the poor. He has sent me to bind up the brokenhearted, to proclaim freedom for the captives and release from darkness for the prisoners, to proclaim the year of the Lord's favour and the day of vengeance of our God, to comfort all who mourn, and provide for those who grieve in Zion-to bestow on them a crown of beauty instead of ashes, the oil of gladness instead of mourning, and a garment of praise instead of a spirit of despair. They will be called oaks of righteousness, a planting of the Lord for the display of his splendour. They will rebuild the ancient ruins and restore the places long devastated; they will renew the ruined cities that have been devastated for generations. (Isaiah 61:1-4)"

Carey resolved that he would take God's Word at its face value, that from those ashes he would have a better press and more scholarly translations. They were able to salvage the five presses, punches, and matrices. And within a few months, Ward had opened a long warehouse nearer the river shore.

Little did these simple scholars know that this fire would prove to be the means of making them and their work famous all over Europe and America as well as in India. In just fifty days about ten thousand pounds were raised in England and Scotland alone, until Andrew Fuller, Carey's friend, supporter, and a BMS leader, returning from his last fund-raising campaign, entered the room of his committee, declaring, "We must stop the contributions." More money had been raised than was needed to cover the losses of the fire. Even in America, people helped generously. In Calcutta, the newspapers caught the enthusiasm, and one leading article concluded with the assurance that the Serampore press would, "like a phoenix of antiquity, rise from its ashes, winged with new strength and destined, in a lofty and long enduring flight, widely to diffuse the benefits of knowledge throughout the East."

After two months, Fuller in England was able to send slips of sheets of the Tamil Testament, printed from these types, to the towns and churches which had subscribed. After six months the whole loss in Oriental types had been recovered. Carey and his two heroic brethren wrote: "We found on making the trail that the advantages of going over the same ground a second time were so great that they fully counter-balanced the time requisite to be devoted thereto in a second translation. The fire, the cause of which was never discovered, and insurance against which did not exist in India, had given birth to revised editions."

Another result was that two missionaries arrived in Serampore— one a professional type-cutter and the other a doctor with his wife, perhaps the first missionary nurse. Dr. Johns was soon to be deported (because he had no licence from the East India Company) just weeks before the renewal of the Company's charter was to be debated in Parliament. Wilberforce tirelessly campaigned with petitions about letting missionaries go to India. In June 1813 the Charter Renewal Bill was amended and included a clause, which came to be known as the "pious clause," stating that it was the duty of Britain "to promote the

interest and happiness" of the Indian people by "taking such measures
... as may tend to the moral improvement" and that "facilities should be
afforded by law to persons wishing to go to India for that purpose." The
first person to be granted that licence was Carey's nephew Eustace.

Trouble never strikes singly: The fire had come after a huge
earthquake, and there had been deaths in each of the seven missionary
families at Serampore. Carey had himself just buried a grandson. Yet
Marshman writes to John Ryland in England, in an SOS:

> "The calamity was another leaf of the ways of Providence, calling
> for the exercise of faith in Him, whose word, firm as the pillars of
> Heaven, has decreed that all things work together for good to them
> that love God. Be strong therefore in the Lord. He will never
> forsake the work of His own hands."

CONFLICTS IN COMMUNITY

Another fire was to burn the heart of Carey, and that was the fire of
contention with his society in England, coupled with his troubles with
the younger missionaries who had joined him. This bitterness
originated in England.

Forbes Jackson says that the greatest trial of a missionary is often
another missionary. This was the case with the five very able and
dedicated men who came to Serampore to assist Carey, but who
temporarily split with him and started the Calcutta Missionary Union.
According to one of his biographers, Carey said that never in his life
"had anything preyed so much upon his spirit as this episode."

This conflict happened at a time when Carey had been grieved by
the loss of his second wife, who had brought such great comfort to his
life. He also had just lost his father and had broken a leg. And his son
Felix had brought great humiliation and embarrassment to him. Felix
had been sent to Burma and now had returned to Calcutta behaving as
though he were the ambassador from Burma. He had delusions of

grandeur and began drinking heavily and adopting a lavish lifestyle. Carey eventually had to repay all the debts that his son incurred.

Carey's colleague William Ward was worn out and in poor health. Marshman was being attacked by the younger missionaries for being autocratic. All three men were feeling the strain of many years in the debilitating climate of Bengal with no home leave, vacation, or relief.

The "pious clause," inserted in the 1813 charter to increase missionary activity and thereby create greater freedom, also brought increased bickering and internal conflicts among the missionaries.[1] Dr. Johns, who had been deported just a few months before Wilberforce's parliamentary victory, criticised Marshman for not trying hard enough to prevent his being deported. This charge emerged just when others were planning to come out to India. False allegations take their toll: This one coloured the perspective of the newcomers.

This happened to have been the time when the mission society was growing rapidly. Two of the "old trio" in England—John Sutcliff and Andrew Fuller—had died (the third member being Dr. John Ryland). They had known Carey personally, encouraged him with letters and money, and coordinated their mission. Nineteen new members who did not know Carey personally had joined the society. They had not been associated with the growing pains of the mission; they did not know why the old guard did things the way they did them.

Of the three, Fuller had been the most faithful supporter and friend to Carey and the mission. This chief apologist of missions had worn himself out to see that the new charter included the "pious clause." He prayed for the mission, raised money, preached, and wrote encouraging letters to Carey. Fuller maintained all along that Serampore should be self-governing because the field staff were better able to govern themselves than the home board could govern them from England—at a time when letters took about six months to arrive.

The mission had become self-supporting because Marshman's schools generated income, which was plowed back into the missionary work. All along, Carey was also giving to the mission from his income in Calcutta. With this self-sufficiency naturally came a fair bit of independence.

The mission in the field had become famous, while its home board's control had weakened. This was inevitable, given the field workers' greater age and experience of India. They knew what would work and what would not, and they knew their own strengths and limitations better than the board at home. So when the new missionaries were leaving for India—glasses coloured by Dr. Johns—the home board was also complaining about its lack of control over Serampore. The misunderstandings were to last for fifteen years. People doubted the integrity of the Serampore missionaries and suspected them of misappropriating funds—this in spite of Carey giving all he had to missions, so much so that he writes, "If I were to die today, I should not leave property enough for the purchase of a coffin and my wife would be entirely unprovided for."

Carey himself gives this amplified description of the charges against him and his colleagues:

"The Serampore Missionaries—Carey, Marshman, and Ward— have acted a dishonest part, alias are rogues. But we do not include Dr. Carey in this charge of dishonesty; he is an easy sort of a man, who will agree to anything for the sake of peace, or in other words he is a fool. Mr. Ward, it is well known, say they, was the tool of Dr. Marshman, but it is gone from the present scene, and it is unlovely to say any evil of the dead."

The crisis came to a head when the committee demanded that all the property at Serampore—schools, printing press, church, and houses—be transferred to the trustees. The Serampore trio refused to meet this demand, further fueling the committee's suspicions. Then the committee sent a printer to assist Ward, directing him to stay at Serampore. But the missionaries, being a closely-knit family, resented this. They preferred to see if the person would fit in with their community over a period of time. Next came Eustace Carey, Carey's nephew, who at first was very appreciative of his uncle's work, but later became critical because of the committee's reports. He also thought the pioneering missionaries were too rigid and autocratic.

The schism it seems was complete when the younger group formed the Calcutta Missionary Union. About this Carey writes,

"I do not recollect in my whole life anything which has given me so much distress as this schism. Many sleepless nights have I spent examining what we have done to give it occasion but can discover nothing on which I can fix. The Mission, however, is rent in twain, and exhibits the scandalous appearance of a body divided against itself."

When asked to join the "Union" and leave Marshman out, Carey said that he was quite aware of Marshman's faults, but his excellencies were such that his defects were almost concealed by them. He said that he despised all attempts to draw him away from his colleague of eighteen years. He was very willing to remove misunderstanding; he would on bended knee ask pardon of anyone he had offended; "that if it was proved that I had either said or done what was wrong, I should count it an honour to acknowledge it, and would do it without hesitation."

Carey's humility, loyalty to his old friends, patience with the younger men, and a deep desire for unity paid off when finally, in 1820, there was reconciliation. The efforts of the older and younger missionaries became tributaries that joined to form one big river of blessing.

In the face of the devastating floods of 1823, Carey showed characteristic and dogged perseverance, a quality he displayed throughout his life in the face of every conceivable discouragement—of which he had more than his share. His school buildings were seriously damaged, his own home destroyed, and his beautiful garden washed away. But now, unlike in 1812 after the fire, there was no help forthcoming from England. Slander had stifled the generosity of the Baptists at home towards the work in Serampore. His own sisters, who had been very close to him, had turned against him. Even his son Jabez was to join the opposition briefly.

After sixteen years of this bitter wrangling, the trio were in abject poverty. No longer was Carey a teacher at Fort William; the Serampore College and Mission had lost all their Indian funds through the collapse of the European banks in Bengal. But the three missionaries were not so much concerned about their personal needs as for the nineteen mission stations that they had to maintain plus other financial commitments Carey had to his family in England. As always in times of distress, the missionaries accepted their plight as a sign of God's chastening.

For two months the nineteen mission stations did not get their allowances, and at last, Carey sent home an appeal for financial support. It could be that these anxieties helped Carey and Marshman to surrender their independence and fall in line with the wishes of the home committee. All the Serampore properties were transferred to the care of eleven trustees in England. All they asked was that they be allowed to stay rent-free for the remainder of their lives. Their plea did not go unheeded; the society sent them a thousand pounds in 1831. Then John Mack rejoined them, and this brought great cheer and encouragement.

Carey was now very ill with a fever that lasted a month: His healing came not just from the finances and the presence of John Mack, but from letters that were for the first time in years gracious and kind.

William Carey died three years later, on June 9, 1834. Robert Hall spoke thus of him:

> "That extraordinary man, who from the lowest obscurity and poverty, without assistance, rose by dint of unrelenting industry to the highest honours of literature, became one of the first of Orientalists, the first of missionaries, and the instrument of diffusing more religious knowledge among his contemporaries than has fallen to the lot of any individual since the Reformation; a man who unites with the most profound and varied attainments the fervour of an evangelist, the piety of a saint and the simplicity of a child."

Footnotes (Chapter 3)

---

[1] The "pious clause" in the 1813 charter of the East India Company was Wilberforce's undertaking, and was drafted by Charles Grant. It sought to ease the way for chaplains and ministers of religion to go to India. The preamble read: "That it is the peculiar and bounden duty of the legislature to promote by all just and prudent means the interests and happiness of the inhabitants of the British Dominions of India and for these ends such measures ought to be adopted as may gradually tend to their advancement in useful knowledge, and to their religious and moral improvement."

Chapter Four

❦

WILLIAM CAREY AND THE MAKING OF MODERN INDIA

WE TURN IN THIS CHAPTER TO SOME OF THE profound contributions of William Carey, and those contemporaries who shared his beliefs, to the process of modernisation in India. Some historians believe that the modernisation of India began on March 7, 1835. On that date, Lord Thomas Babbington Macaulay advocated in his famous "Minute on Education" that the East India Company ought to use its grant for public instruction, for English education.

If, however, we begin to ask simple questions such as, Who was Macaulay? Who and what influenced his decision? What enabled him to overrule the great Orientalists who advocated the teaching of Sanskrit, Persian, and Arabic? Why was this money available in the first place? What exactly did he mean by "English" education? How did he foresee his Minute being carried out? We would quickly come to the conclusion that Macaulay's Minute actually was the culmination of a process started by William Carey in 1792.

William Carey's contributions to India's modernisation have not been adequately appreciated. Sadly, some scholars even undermine them. The process of India's reform has already been halted, and in some important respects, Indian society seems to be reverting to its old evils. We must look not so much at Carey himself, but at the beliefs he shared with others, that led to the reforms being initiated.

But first, we need to be rid of the idea that India's contact with England automatically resulted in reform, an idea rooted not in the evidence of history, but in a blind faith in the doctrine of social evolution, which wrongly holds that societies inevitably evolve and improve.

We need also to get a bird's-eye view of the people and processes that lay behind the reforms.

THE BRITISH TEMPER TOWARD INDIA
AT THE TIME OF CAREY

Almost until the arrival of Lord William Cavendish Bentinck in 1828 as the governor-general, when the evangelical influence over the East India Company was at its peak, the mainstream British attitude toward India did not favor a struggle for its improvement; British involvement in India, it had been felt, should be kept to a minimum.

This view was shaped by three major interests. For the *directors of the East India Company*, India was simply a trading base—as it had been since England first began trading there in the early 1600s. Most of these merchants did not even want to govern India, let alone assume the responsibility of reforming it. For example, their simple commercial minds found Lord Wellesley's empire-building military successes too much for their ledgers, so he was recalled.

Lord Macaulay, an outstanding historian of the nineteenth century, described the East India Company during the initial phase of its rule in Bengal as "a gang of public robbers." Robert Clive, who in the mid-1700s won Bengal for the Company, had himself taken a bribe of two hundred thousand pounds from the puppet he installed as the nawab. The Company's greed was a major factor that, within the first fifty years of its power, helped destroy India's two-thousand-year-old economic strength. This strength had been built on trade and industry, especially the weaving industry. Factors such as casteism, feudalism, illiteracy, inequality of male and female, absence of a fair legal system, and (Mogul/Maratha, Sikh and Hindu) imperialism ensured that the benefits of the economy did not percolate down to the average person, who therefore had little interest in defending the socioeconomic system when it was attacked by foreigners.

For the *British military men* such as Clive and Wellesley, India was primarily so much "territory to be conquered." This attitude ensured that, even though Wellesley was convinced of the rightness of Carey's campaign against *sati* in 1806, he did not issue an edict against it, as Bentinck later did in 1829.

The *British intellectuals and humanitarians* in India, such as Sir Thomas Munro and Sir John Malcolm, tended merely to respect and romanticise the "customs and wisdom of the natives." The British Orientalists patronised Sanskrit and rediscovered the greatness of ancient Indian literature, which helped to revive the self-respect of the Indian elite. Their efforts, however, could do nothing to reform the Indian populace. On the contrary, it appeared that they were reinforcing the religious basis for some of the social evils. Raja Ram Mohun Roy—himself a great Sanskrit scholar—severely condemned the attempt of the British Orientalists to start a Sanskrit college in Calcutta, which would have further solidified the existing class distinctions.

For decades the British had a policy of not employing Indians for responsible administrative positions. They believed that Indians were dishonest and could not be trusted. Although both Munro and Malcolm also agreed that Indians were dishonest, they nevertheless argued against this policy of discrimination. They thought that if the Indian elite were paid on a par with the British, they too might become morally upright. Nonetheless, they ruled out the possibility that

Indians could be reformed. Munro, who was governor of Madras from 1820–24, wrote on June 30, 1821:

> "I have no faith in the modern doctrine of the rapid improvement of the Hindoos, or of any other people. The character of the Hindoos is probably much the same as when Vasco da Gama first visited India, and it is not likely that it will be much better a century hence.
>
> When I read, as I sometimes do, of a measure by which a large province had been suddenly improved, or a race of semi-barbarians, civilised, almost to Quakerism, I throw away the book."

A MINORITY WITH A MISSIONARY VISION

Those reformers who advocated this "modern doctrine of the rapid improvement of the Hindoos" were the "fourth force" in England's policy toward India. They were only a tiny minority at the end of the eighteenth century, but, in contrast to the other three viewpoints, they argued for the maximum possible British involvement in India in the mutual interest of both England and India.

It should be obvious that the reformation and modernisation of India had to be the work, primarily, of those who both loved India and were not blind to its faults. A reformer has to have some basis for believing that even the most degenerate person can be saved; some basis for hope that good can triumph over evil, that a whole society oppressed by ignorance and "wickedness" for thousands of years can be transformed, almost miraculously, without the use of force.

THE POWER OF TWO PENS

Let us look briefly at two books and their authors who began the modernisation of India. One, Charles Grant, worked behind the scenes in England, while the other, William Carey, laboured in the heat and dust of India.

These reformers began to articulate their views one year before the British Parliament was to renew the East India Company's charter in 1793.

Charles Grant had served with the Company for thirteen years in India and had seen the evils both of the Company and of India's populace. He believed that both needed to be changed. William Carey had gathered his knowledge of the world and of India from a careful study of history and the reports of travelers such as Captain Cook.

Carey's book was written in 1791 and published in 1792. Grant's was written in 1792 and published in 1797, and, even before it was published, managed to influence the parliamentary debate on India of 1793. After his book was reprinted as a state paper in 1812, it became the then most widely read statement on India. By then Grant was both a member of Parliament and one of the top brass of the East India Company.

Charles Grant's Observations

Charles Grant's book, which began to influence the reformers' minds, including that of Lord Macaulay's father, had an elongated title: *Observations on the State of Society among the Asiatic Subjects of Great Britain, particularly with respect to Morals and on the Means of Improving it. Written Chiefly in the Year 1792.*

Grant was a member of the famous evangelical group, the "Clapham Sect." He was a close friend of its leader, William Wilberforce—the evangelical member of Parliament who was then fighting a battle that was to last till the end of his life, against the British law that allowed its chartered companies to buy and sell African slaves. Grant began to look at India differently from the way his colleagues in the East India Company viewed the colony, primarily because of his conversion to evangelical Christianity in 1790, two years before he wrote his book.

The word *conversion* has come to acquire negative connotations because of the belief that all truth is *relative*, and all beliefs valid. In England, in Grant's day, changing one's religion or religious beliefs was not the primary meaning of conversion. According to the evangelicals, every baptised person, called "Christian," also needed to be converted, i.e., needed to repent of sin and be transformed by the power of the Holy Spirit, through faith in Jesus Christ. (The word *evangelical* was initially used for those Anglicans who believed the Bible to be God's Word and emphasised the necessity of personal conversion. Later, the word began to be used to describe all Christians who shared that belief.)

For Grant himself, to be converted meant that even though he was a businessman, he no longer lived for making money, but for honouring the Lord Jesus Christ. That, in turn, meant that he could no longer look at the Indian people with the eyes of a merchant—a people to be exploited for economic gain —but instead, he looked from Christ's perspective: Indians had to be loved and served, as Jesus would have done. An interesting and tangible proof of Grant's conversion is that upon his death in 1824, he left his legacy to William Carey. All the wealth he had earned from India through the East India Company was reinvested in India's modernisation. The sincerity of his heart is also authenticated by the fact that his son, also named Charles Grant, put his reforming ideas into the 1833 charter of the East India Company. His other son, Robert Grant, who also went back to serve India, composed the famous hymn, "O Worship the King, All Glorious Above."

In order to be converted, Grant had to acknowledge and then repent of the sin in his own life. It also meant he could neither overlook nor excuse the evil habits of the people of India. As a practical man of commerce (unlike many theoreticians of today), he realised that moral poverty could cause a great country to sink into chronic misery:

"Upon the whole, then, we cannot avoid recognising in the people of Hindostan, a race of men lamentably degenerate and base; retaining but a feeble sense of moral obligation . ... governed by malevolent and licentious passions, strongly exemplifying the effects produced on society by a great and general corruption of manners, and sunk in misery by their vices, in a country peculiarly calculated by its natural advantages, to promote the prosperity of its inhabitants."

William Carey's Enquiry

Many people today understandably detest the very title of Carey's *An Enquiry into the Obligations of Christians to Use Means for the Conversion of the Heathen*. The words *heathen* and *conversion* have acquired negative and repulsive connotations.

However, all the great social reformers in nineteenth-century India accepted Carey's belief that, in many cases, conversion—or the change of one's character and false beliefs—was the only effective means of social reform. The proliferation of new religious sects that followed Carey testifies to the compelling power of Carey's conviction. The better-known examples of these sects are: the Brahma Samaj (Ram Mohun Roy), the *Prarthna Samaj* (Keshub Chandra Sen), the *Satya Shodhak Samaj* (Jotiba Phule), the *Arya Samaj* (Swami Dayanand) and the *Ramakrishna Mission* (Vivekananda), which is still fighting a legal battle demanding that it should be classified as a religion separate from Hinduism. This belief that conversion is a key to reform continued well into this century, at least until 1956 when Dr. B. R. Ambedkar converted to Buddhism with his half million followers. The reasons for the perceived connection between conversion and reform will become clear shortly.

If you read Carey's *Enquiry* you will find that Carey was "inquiring" into the question of whether or not Christians were under an obligation (in light of Christ's commands) to help transform societies that live in intellectual, moral, social, political, and spiritual darkness.

We have pointed out that we cannot even think of reforming a society unless we first acknowledge it to be needing reform, however sophisticated a name we choose to give to a society in the grip of moral decadence. For example, militant Hindu forces fighting for a *Ram Rajya* are implicitly acknowledging that India is a kingdom of a demon god—Ravana.[1] During Carey's time, such aspirations warranted the adjective *heathen*.

Carey was recognised as a "friend of India," yet he saw no problem in using the word *heathen*. It was the word an educated Englishman used in a descriptive rather than a derogatory sense. Today we would describe India with phrases such as "third world," "underdeveloped" or "a developing country"; where we now see things in economic and technological terms alone, Carey saw the moral and philosophical roots of economic backwardness. As a matter of fact, even the economists of that day perceived themselves primarily as moral philosophers. Adam Smith's work, for example, implied that the British government in India had to submit an annual report entitled "Moral and Material Progress in India."

HOW CAN A SOCIETY BE TRANSFORMED MORALLY?

Carey did not agree with the Humanists such as Sir Munro, who felt that the moral improvement of the people of "Hindostan" was impossible. He believed, in obedience to Christ's command to "go into all the world and preach the good news," that reform, even dramatic improvement, was possible because God wanted to save human beings from their bondage to sin and Satan.

Carey's belief in the possibility of reform was rooted in his careful study of history—both biblical and secular. The second section of his *Enquiry*, for example, refers to an impressive list of well-documented stories of Christian preachers and missionaries who were his models. These include Peter, Paul, and the other apostles in the first century; Justin Martyr in the middle of the second century; Irenaeus around A.D. 170; Tertullian twenty years later; Frumentius at the time of Constantine; Moses in 372; Palladius in 432; Austin in 596; Amandus in 589; Egidius in 648; Willifred in 684; Chilianus in 688; Charlemagne in 800; Ansgarius in 833; Methodius in 861; Wycliffe in 1369, followed by Hus, Jerome, Luther, Calvin, Melanchthon, and Bucer, all of whose works led to the great European Reformation. Then there were Elliot in 1632; Ziegenbalg in 1706; and Brainerd in 1743. And finally, of course, there was Wesley, the impact of whose preaching had saved England from a bloody revolution such as the one in France—which for Carey's readers needed no documentation, for the French Revolution was happening as he wrote.

William Carey knew firsthand what social scientists such as Max Weber later documented, that politically and economically strong countries (such as Germany, Switzerland, Holland, and England) had been transformed by the preaching of Reformers such as Martin Luther and John Calvin. Carey reasoned that what God could do for the once-barbarous Britons and the once-heathen Europe, he was able to accomplish anywhere. As he wrote in his *Enquiry*:

"The uncivilised state of the heathen, instead of affording an objection *against* preaching the Gospel to them, ought to furnish an argument *for* it. Can we as men, or as Christians, hear that a great part of our fellow creatures, whose souls are as immortal as ours, and who are as capable as us ... are enveloped in ignorance and barbarism? Can we hear that they are without the Gospel, without government, without laws, and without arts and sciences, and not exert ... ourselves to introduce amongst them the sentiments of men, and of Christians? Would not the spread of the Gospel be the most effectual means of their civilisation? Would not that make them useful members of society? We know that such effects did in a measure follow the afore-mentioned efforts of Elliot, Brainerd, and others amongst the American Indians."

THREE PRESUPPOSITIONS OF CAREY'S REFORMS

It is easy to miss seeing, or to misunderstand, some basic assumptions of Carey's work, because the mentality of our day is so different from his.

First, today, in a country such as India, every champion of the poor or the downtrodden sees himself as a savior or a mini-messiah. Carey, in contrast, did not see himself as a savior. For him, salvation was God's work. A reformer's primary duty was to pray. He wrote: "One of the first, and most important of those duties which are incumbent upon us, is *fervent and united prayer.*"

This understanding that transforming mankind was the work of God, sounds alien today, but for 150 years it remained Carey's abiding legacy to all the reformers of India, not only for the Christian but also for his "Hindu" successors—from Raja Ram Mohun Roy at the beginning of the nineteenth century, to Mahatma Gandhi, who was assassinated while on his way to a prayer meeting.

While many of the Indian reformers did not accept Carey's Trinitarian God, most of them, nonetheless, were forced through influence such as his to believe in a theistic God who is infinite—personal and sovereign and active in human history-one who answers prayers. These reformers recognised that neither the impersonal deity of philosophic Hinduism, nor the finite gods of folk Hinduism were adequate for the needs of sinful human societies. The former could not respond to prayers and the latter—gods and goddesses of mythology—were subject to the same human failings as ourselves. Carey believed that prayer makes a difference, not just in our minds but also in our history because that was the essence of the Gospel: In Jesus, the

Messiah, the Sovereign Lord had entered human history as the "Light of the world."

Carey's second assumption was that creation was rational, not magical or mystical. He placed great emphasis on introducing modern science to India. He himself taught zoology, botany, and astronomy—in addition to theology—in his college at Serampore.

Some Indian intellectuals are espousing postmodernism because it seems to vindicate the traditional Hindu rejection of rational order, initially propagated by Adi Shankaracharya. This revival of anti-rational religion in India undermines the scientific temper that reformers, beginning with Carey, tried to plant.

For our purposes here, it is sufficient to point out that Carey spent enormous energy in translating and promoting the Bible because as a modern man, he believed that God's revelation alone could remove superstition and inculcate confidence in human rationality—a prerequisite for the modernisation of India.

Our generation has also tried to banish a third basic idea of Carey's, which was central to his understanding of how lasting reforms can take place: his concept of *conversion*. Two factors need to be understood here.

William Carey shared Charles Grant's belief that our moral rebellion is at the root of our human problems. Human misery is neither a result of *avidhya* (ignorance of our divinity), nor is it a product of *kama* (desire). It is a result of human refusal to live under the moral authority of our heavenly Father. Carey believed that it is the duty of reformers to share with everyone the blessings of "conversion," of renewed fellowship with God. According to his study of history, conversion, reform, and modernisation were intimately related processes. Carey believed that by preaching and by translating and publishing the Bible in Indian vernaculars, he was laying the foundation stone for India's modernisation.

There is a second profound (and still relevant) factor that made Carey see conversion as the basis of reform. According to the British political doctrine of religious liberty, the state was not allowed to interfere with the religious conscience of the people. If social evils such as untouchability were the results of religious beliefs, then they had to be countered by true and better beliefs in equal human dignity—not merely by legislation or administrative force. Some of the greatest Indian minds of the nineteenth century understood and appreciated the missionary effort to "convert" Indians. This is how Keshub Chandra Sen, the successor of Raja Ram Mohun Roy and the founder of the *Prarthna Samaj*, reacted to the missionary work:

> "We breathe, think, feel, move in a Christian atmosphere under the influence of Christian education; the whole mature society is awakened, enlightened, reformed ... our hearts have been touched, conquered, subjugated by a superior power and that power is Christ. Christ rules British India, and not the British Government. England has sent us a tremendous moral force, in the life and character of that mighty prophet, to conquer and hold this vast empire. None but Jesus ever deserved this bright, precious diadem—India—and Christ shall have it."

The British government, of course, had not sent the missionaries; but the evangelicals needed to reform the East India Company and the British Parliament before they could get permission for their task of reforming India.

REFORMING THE BRITISH PARLIAMENT

The influence these evangelicals exerted on Britain was much greater than in India. Within England they were better understood; their motives were less suspect, and their efforts were backed by thousands of unknown and unsung clergymen. What they had hoped to achieve in India is, two centuries later, still incomplete, substantially because secular humanism has undermined what the Christians were seeking to do.

William Wilberforce was the chief spokesman for Grant and Carey inside the British Parliament. He forcefully presented their arguments that England must assume the responsibility of "uplifting" India and believed that the chief problem of India's people was immorality and superstition in the guise of religion.

The doctrine of religious liberty had already come to have two implications: One was that the power of the state should not be used to tamper with the religious conscience of the people. If a social evil such as untouchability or destructive superstitions such as astrology had overt religious sanction, then the state could not erase them by force or by legislation.

The other implication of the doctrine of religious liberty was that the removal of these religiously sanctioned evils had to be the work of counter-reforming religious (or non-religious) ideas. All ideas had to be given the freedom to compete in the marketplace of ideas to change people's beliefs and, thereby, their society.

Wilberforce argued that England should send Christian missionaries who could help "improve" Indian society. In 1793 he succeeded in pushing his proposals through the House of Commons, but unfortunately, the House of Lords overthrew his proposals. Despite this official rejection, Carey's sense of a divine call gave him the inner strength to set out for India that same year.

It took twenty years of successful fieldwork by Carey in India, lobbying within the East India Company by Charles Grant, and magnificent political work by Wilberforce in England, to persuade the Parliament in 1813 (when the charter came up for renewal) to begin to assume its moral obligation to India.

William Carey's persistence paid off when William Wilberforce, whose proposals had failed in the British Parliament a second time in

1795, once again took up the issue in 1813. This time Wilberforce was
backed by the documentation supplied by Carey and others, such as
Rev. Claudius Buchanan, vice-provost of Fort William College. These
facts included lists of widows who had committed *sati*. Wilberforce had
made a practice of reading out their names at his dining table and
praying for India. On June 22, 1813, Wilberforce argued before
Parliament:

> "Christianity, independently of its effects on a future state of
> existence (i.e., heaven), has been acknowledged even by avowed
> skeptics, to be, beyond all other institutions that ever existed,
> favourable to the temporal interests and happiness of man: And
> never was there a country where there is a greater need than in India
> for the diffusion of its genial influence."

He continued his arguments on the first and twelfth of July:

> "Let us endeavour to strike our roots into the soil by the gradual
> introduction and establishment of our own principles and
> opinions; of our laws, institutions, and manners; above all, as the
> source of every other improvement, of our religion, and
> consequently of our morals."

Wilberforce said that such a reforming effort, and not brute military
force or political intrigue, would tie India to England with bonds of
eternal gratitude.

The critics suggested that, through his advocacy of allowing
missionaries to propagate Christianity in India, Wilberforce was
counseling compulsory conversion. He rebutted the charge:

> "Compulsion and Christianity! Why the very terms are at variance
> with each other—the ideas are incompatible. In the language of
> Inspiration itself, Christianity has been called the "law of liberty."

We should note two facts about the idea of religious pluralism. First, it
was this commitment to the doctrine of the religious neutrality of the

state that shaped Carey's arguments against *sati* in 1805–1806. The crux of his argument was that *sati* was not a religious practice enjoined by the Hindu scriptures, and therefore it could be banned by the government without violating the principle of separation of religion and state. A decade later, Raja Ram Mohun Roy was to use the same argument—since the only defence of the pro-*sati* lobby was that *sati* was a religious practice. It should also be noted that it was this spirit of administrative tolerance toward socioreligious practices, even when they were obviously evil, that later became the basis of the policy of religious pluralism in independent India. Pluralism, another feature of modernisation, is also under a serious threat today as India turns away from the legacy of the reformers.

Carey's generation, in contrast to our own, believed that it was possible for us to know the truth because God had revealed it: in nature, in history, and also in the Bible. Carey was committed to pluralism... to the idea that the state should not support one religious belief over another. He believed that it was the responsibility of the individual to discover the revealed truth—in both the scientific and the historical spheres, as well as in the theological sphere. For example, is it true that some people are born untouchables because of their *karma*, or is it a lie, perpetuated by a class of people in their own self-interest?

Carey's generation believed that it was necessary for us to freely dialogue and debate truth because we all tend to believe rationalisations that are untrue. Freedom of conscience is incomplete without the freedom to change one's beliefs, to convert. A state that hinders conversion is uncivilised because it restricts the human quest for truth and reform.

In politics, however, arguments alone are rarely enough. Wilberforce had already tasted defeat in Parliament more than once. In 1813 he took the precaution of mobilising public pressure, particularly pressure on the House of Lords. The unsuspecting Lords were swept off their feet by the strength of public opinion. Historians acknowledge that public opinion, on which Wilberforce capitalised, was substantially a result of the publicity Carey's work had generated in England during the previous two decades. The impact of this work was greatly reinforced by books by Grant. Buchanan's well-received book, *The Christian Researches in Asia*, gave a vivid firsthand account of the horrors associated with the Jagannath festival in Puri.[2]

For India, two immediate positive results of this parliamentary victory were: a) the East India Company had to allow missionaries freedom to work, and b) the Company was asked to earmark Rs. 100,000 annually from its profits for public education in India. The consequence of the former was that great missionary educators such as Alexander Duff could freely come to India and open schools and colleges; the consequence of the latter was Macaulay's Minute, twenty-two years later, which determined how this money, available since 1813, was to be used.

It took twenty years of struggle (to the time of the next renewal of the Company's charter in 1833), before the reformers' viewpoint really began to determine British policy. But the foundations had been laid.

REFORMING THE COMPANY

Charles Grant knew that the greatest obstacle to the missionary endeavor of helping to reform India was his own East India Company. The Company, in turn, knew (partly from Grant's own writing, and also from the headache Wilberforce was giving to the Company's counterpart in Africa), that the missionaries would disturb the Company's profitable activities by stirring up the native peoples. Carey, for example, was known to be a potential troublemaker. While still in England he had been opposed even to using the sugar made by slave labour and imported by British companies.

Grant resolved to attempt the reform of the East India Company by becoming the leader of the reformers' assault on the Company's board.

His first victory came in 1805–1806 when he managed to send five "serious" (reform-minded, evangelical) clergymen to India as chaplains for the Company, to try to reform its employees. One of these five was the renowned Henry Martyn, who spent his first months in India with Carey, and, under Carey's influence, went on to create Hindustani as a modern literary language through his translation of the New Testament. It was the Hindustani created by Henry Martyn, Rev. Gilchrist, and the others at Fort William College, out of which came the modern Hindi and Urdu—the national languages of India and Pakistan.

Grant's victory, in a substantial measure, was a result of Carey's success in India. In 1800, Lord Wellesley had already been forced to invite Carey to teach Bengali to the administrators of the Company in Fort William College. Today it seems incredible that in Calcutta—not in Kashmir, not in Kerala, but in Calcutta, the very capital of Bengal—they could not find a teacher of Bengali. This was sufficient proof that a missionary had a much greater motivation to identify with the people of India than had either the learned Indian pundits or the British rulers. William Carey's appointment gave him an opportunity to break down the anti-missionary prejudices of the Company's top brass.

Under Grant, the evangelical infiltration of the East India Company and the takeover of its directorate was so spectacular that historian Ian Bradley can say, "There was no year between 1807 and 1830 when either the Chairman or the Deputy Chairman of the Board of Directors was not an Evangelical."

Many Indian historians don't seem to know that Lord Bentinck began to lend overt administrative support to the reforms because he too was one of the many official's evangelicals had deliberately "planted" in the higher echelons of the East India Company to "civilise" India by transforming the Company. Bentinck's friendship with the utilitarian philosophers is well-known, but few seem to know that he was an ardent disciple of Charles Grant. He, too, believed that the Company's first job in India could not be to make money: "The first duty of the Imperial Government is the moral regeneration of the immense mass of our fellow creatures."

Other evangelicals in the leadership of the Company included famous administrators such as John Lawrence, Sir Herbert Edwards, Sir John Nicholson, and Sir Robert Montgomery. These were the men who helped build the modern Punjab as the showpiece of colonial administration. Later, even critics of the evangelicals within the British Raj were grateful that the excellent work of the Christian administrators ensured that the Sikhs stayed out of the 1857 "Mutiny," guaranteeing its failure. Today Indian historians blame the Sikhs for being traitors because they did not participate in India's "First War of Independence." The "blame," in fact, belongs to those builders of modern India. Their excellent work made Sikhs then think that India's interests at that point in history were being better served by these reformer-administrators than by the feudal lords fighting for their own rule.

CAREY'S TWO MOST IMPORTANT CONTRIBUTIONS TO REFORM

We can now turn to the two contributions of William Carey which are of special significance today.

First Contribution: It Is Possible!

The primary presupposition of any reform, as we have already noticed, is that before we can improve a society, we have to admit that it is degenerate. The second presupposition is that a fundamental change is, in fact, possible—even if the majority is against the change. The opposition to Carey was phenomenal. It came from the British Parliament, from the Company, from the military, from the Oriental scholars, from his own mission board, and also from the very people he was seeking to serve—the Indians themselves.

For the 200 years since Carey's day—until fairly recently—it has been taken for granted, at least in theory, that reform is possible. But for two thousand years before Carey the Hindu/Buddhist leadership in India had taught, and the masses had believed, that this earth was a place where souls were sent to take the consequences of their previous *karma* (deeds). Therefore, the meaning of human life, by definition, was suffering. Thus life without suffering was not possible. The only way to escape this prison of suffering was by escaping from life itself—which is the Indian concept of salvation, or *nirvana*.

What, then, should a person born "untouchable" do? Or a widow? Or a leper? The Hindu/Buddhist answer is that all have to live with their *karma* and *dharma* (duties of one's caste), as best they can, without seeking to change fate in any fundamental way.

If we add to this Hindu fatalism (produced by the doctrines of *karma*, reincarnation, and *dharma*) the all-pervasive belief that our life on earth is determined by the astrological deities above, or by the demons and demigods below, then we can begin to understand why scholars such as Sir Thomas Munro had ruled out the possibility of reform. This was not all; if *karma*, stars, and demons did leave some freedom for a person, it was severely limited by the Hindu scriptures, written, often, from Brahmanical self-interest.

We have seen that the Brahmanical scriptural mandates behind India's social and intellectual evils worked powerfully against reforms. Even if an individual British officer believed some Hindu customs to be wicked, he could not use the power of the state against those customs. Is reform possible when religion defends evil and the state is committed not to interfere with religion? Carey's faith in a transcendent Ruler, the

God of History who was above human rulers, sustained him against all odds.

One result of Carey's success has been that, since his day, most Indians (including even those who believe in *karma*, reincarnation, astrology, Brahmanical scriptures, etc.) now tend to agree that reform is possible. They are forced to reject the fatalistic idea that reform is not possible. That premise had ruled Indian civilisation and ruined India for two thousand years. Carey's belief that human suffering can be and should be resisted has dominated the last two hundred years of Indian history.

Today, however, it seems certain that we cannot take it for granted that this optimistic idea will continue to be the mainstream belief. At a theoretical level, Western postmodernism has already rejected the ideas of "progress" and "development" as mythical "meta-narratives." The stage is set for the older Indian pessimism and fatalism to win over the earlier optimism in the twenty-first century, undoing much of what Carey and the reformers who followed him had achieved. For example, in his popular book *The Degeneration of India*, the chief election commissioner, T. N. Seshan, argues that "India is terminally sick." His pessimistic diagnosis is widely believed because few people have done as much as he has to try and cleanse our public life of its all-pervasive corruption. This growing pessimism makes it urgent for us to understand Carey's optimistic mindset.

William Carey believed in the possibility of reform because the Bible taught that the Creator did not intend life to be suffering. God created Adam and Eve to live in Eden—in bliss.

Suffering came later, as a result of sin. Suffering is thus a historical fact, not a metaphysical truism—which means it can be and should be resisted.

Sin is not *karma*. The idea of *karma* is that an impersonal law rules our destiny and automatically gives us the consequences of our actions.

According to the Bible, sin is breaking the laws of a Person—our loving heavenly Father. Therefore, it is possible to find forgiveness and to be delivered from sin and its consequences.

It was this non-humanistic, transcendent faith that sustained Carey and helped him to liberate India from its two-millennia-long bondage to fatalism and religious escapism.

Second Contribution: The Language of Modernisation

Carey's second great contribution to the cause of India's modernisation (which is currently being undermined, partly because it is inadequately understood), is his contribution to the development of India's vernacular languages.

Crucial to the European Protestant Reformers such as Martin Luther was the knowledge that, in order to transform His people, Christ used the language of the common man, Aramaic, rather than the Hebrew of the sacred Jewish Scriptures. Until the sixteenth century, "the languages of learning" and therefore of the elite had been Latin and Greek, whereas ordinary people in Europe spoke German, French, or English. This allowed the privileged elite to exploit ignorance.

In order to liberate the masses, to make the knowledge of the truth available to all the people, the Reformers began to translate the Bible into the languages of the common people. Martin Luther himself translated the Bible into German.

Obviously, to have the Scriptures translated into the spoken language of the people is of little value if they don't read and write the language they speak. Therefore, the Reformers followed Bible translation with a drive to give basic education to the masses. The growth of democracy and market economy in the West became possible as two of the several lasting results of their mission. It is not possible to have a government of the people, by the people, and for the people that functions mainly in the language of the elite. Nor is a genuine market economy possible without the spoken language of the people becoming also the language of learning, science, industry, and the marketplace. The genius of the market economy is that it liberates the energies of the masses for making contributions to the economic life of the country. This is impossible if an elitist language becomes a barrier over which ordinary citizens cannot climb.

Thus, a key factor in modernisation, which Carey tried to popularise, is that the spoken language of the people should also be the language of learning, the language of industry, of marketing, and governing. India has not yet taken this lesson to heart. That is one reason it has been left way behind by countries such as Japan and South Korea, whose modernisation began almost a century after India's.

A feature of medieval society is its use of an elitist language (such as Latin, Persian, Sanskrit, or now, English) as a means of discriminating and also as a method of granting unearned privileges to an aristocracy. It became possible for India to make the transition from Persian as the court language, to Urdu, and then to the regional languages (at least in the lower courts) because of Carey's labour and leadership in turning the vernaculars into literary languages through Bible translation.

This should help us to understand why a reformer such as William Carey was so obsessed with translating and/or publishing the Bible in almost forty different languages, and why he helped start more than one hundred vernacular schools; and why he launched the first college in Asia to teach in an Asian language—Bengali. Their passion for reforming India, by making the Bible available in the vernaculars, motivated the missionaries to develop the grammar for many Indian dialects, and, eventually, to develop Hindi as a literary language for the majority of the citizens of India.

George Smith, one of William Carey's biographers, explains Carey's passion for the vernaculars thus:

"Like the growth of a tree is the development of a language.... In countries like India and China, where civilisation has long ago reached its highest level, and has been declining for want of the salt of a universal Christianity, it is the missionary again who interferes for the highest ends, but by a different process. Mastering the complex classical speech and literature of the learned and priestly class, and living with his Master's sympathy among the people whom that class oppresses, he takes the popular dialects which are instinct with the life of the future; where they are wildly luxuriant he brings them under law, where they are barren he enriches them from the parent stock so as to make them the vehicle of ideas such as Greek gave to Europe, and in time he brings to birth nations worthy of the name by a national language and literature lighted up with the ideas of the Book which he is the first to translate."

Today Bengali—the national language of Bangladesh—is the only Indian language that has the pride of earning a Nobel Prize for literature, for Rabindranath Tagore's *Gitanjali*. But we have already seen that merely ten decades before Tagore, his own city of Calcutta—the capital of Bengal-did not have one qualified teacher of Bengali. This should not be surprising, for the medieval-minded pundits considered Bengali a language "fit only for women and demons." S. K. De points out in his study, *Bengali Literature in the Nineteenth Century*, that it was Carey and his missionary colleagues who "raised the language from the debased condition of an unsettled dialect to the character of a regular and permanent form of speech." The Bengali songs of the *Gitanjali* display both the influence on the language of Carey as well as the worldview of the Bible, which Carey translated.

It is instructive to read why Carey refused to have English as the medium of instruction in the college he founded at Serampore. The following is an excerpt from the Mission report in 1818:

"[The missionaries] apprehended that such a step, [introduction of an English-medium education] in the first instance, would go towards frustrating the very design of the institution. The moment a native youth found he had enough English to enable him to copy an English letter, a stop would have been put to his studies .... They imagined there was a prospect of them getting Rs. 16 or 20 monthly as English copyists in the metropolis. This course, therefore, instead of promoting the welfare of the country would have transformed its finest youth into mercenary copyists, ignorant of their own language and even of English as to any purpose of mental improvement."

Carey's educational efforts, very self-consciously, were directed toward an improvement of the Indian mind, not toward preparing an army of mercenaries for the British Raj. Therefore, he insisted on imparting knowledge in the language of the people, while the Company was already teaching English to prepare its army of hirelings. The efforts of the East India Company would never have produced a Tagore; the missionary effort did.

An additional result of the development of Indian languages was the development of Indian nationalism. Modern nationalism had developed in Europe after the Protestant Reformation, along with the growth of national languages. Carey and the other missionaries knew that a tiny British army had been able to colonise a great country such as India, only because Hinduism had not been able to cultivate a spirit of patriotism in India.

While some later missionaries were undoubtedly racists and others prostituted themselves to the Raj, overall the missionaries came to India because they loved India, and they tried to cultivate, among their converts, patriotism or a love for India. Their efforts began to succeed after they persuaded Michael Madhusudan Dutt—an upper-caste convert—to write his poetry in Bengali and not only in English. It was Dutt's poetry that triggered what is often called the "Bengali Renaissance" or the Bengali Nationalism. It produced Bankim Chandra

Chatterjee, Swami Vivekananda, Rabindranath Tagore, and finally Mahatma Gandhi.

Carey was well aware that the Indian languages were not developed enough to translate European knowledge into them or to use them as media for higher education. Nor did they have the necessary literature. He strove therefore to develop both the vernacular languages and their literature. After a team of pundits would complete a translation of the Bible in a vernacular, he would encourage them to begin translating educational books in that same language. This work, unfortunately, was necessarily a slow process during his lifetime. Neither the Indian elite nor the East India Company provided Carey with either resources or work partners who shared his vision. The missionary societies who later, following Carey's initiative, did motivate thousands of men and women to give to India their lives and resources, at that time were just getting off the ground. Countries such as Japan and South Korea have made great advances over India, partly because they immediately translate almost every book that is worth anything.

MACAULAY'S MINUTE AND "ENGLISH" EDUCATION

Lord Macaulay's Minute served as a rocket booster, launching into a sustained orbit the educational revolution of India. Few Indian historians, however, seem to know that the man immediately behind Macaulay's Minute was Carey's younger contemporary, Alexander Duff, a close friend of Macaulay's brother-in-law, Charles Trevelyan. Duff, who under Carey's inspiration pioneered English education in Calcutta, also started the controversy between an Oriental and an English education for India. Macaulay was asked to help resolve that controversy.

Carey had encouraged Duff to start educational institutions that imparted European education. Carey's thesis was that European education should be the substance, with the vernacular language as its medium or vehicle. Duff agreed with Carey, but he found that the youth in Calcutta were more interested in learning English than in learning the vernacular. Besides this problem, of course, the poverty of the Indian mind had ensured that the literature for higher education did not exist in the vernacular. Duff was a linguist who knew that developing vernaculars such as German and English unleashed the energy of the masses that developed Europe. Nevertheless, he felt that in his day they still needed to use English as the medium for instruction. Knowledge of English would make it possible for future generations of Indians to love India enough to produce the vernacular literature to help modernise thinking India. Duff wrote:

> "I saw clearly and expressed myself strongly to the effect that ultimately, in a generation or two, the Bengalee, by improvement might become the fitting medium for European knowledge. But at that time it was a poor language, like English before Chaucer, and had in it, neither by translation nor original composition, no works embodying any subjects of study beyond the merest elements."

After Lord Macaulay had ruled in favor of "English" education, Alexander Duff had the following to say about the choice between English and the vernacular, clearly displaying Carey's influence on his thinking:

> "Who, then, will hesitate in affirming that, in the meantime, the Government has acted wisely in appointing the English language as the medium of communicating English literature and science to the select youth of India? And who will venture to say that the wisdom of the act would be diminished if it guaranteed the continuance of English as the medium until the living spoken dialects of India became ripened, by the copious infusion of expressive terms, for the formation of a new and improved national literature?"

The wisdom of Macaulay's act, unfortunately, has been diminished today. Contrary to the expectations of the pioneers of India's reform,

English has simply replaced Sanskrit as the language of the learned elite. It has become the language of unfair discrimination and unearned privilege, driving India back towards medievalism.

India's medieval mindset has misunderstood Macaulay's advocacy of an "English" education.

To begin with, we need to know that Duff and Macaulay were not discussing the relative merits of English and the vernacular, but the relative merits of Oriental education versus English or European education.

The chief Orientalists, who were called the Brahmanising Five (the Hon. H. Shakespeare, H. Thoby Prinsep, James Prinsep, William Hay Macnaghten, and T. C. C. Sutherland) had ensured that the Company's grant of Rs.100,000 would be used for promoting the knowledge of Sanskrit, Persian, and Arabic. This was in spite of the fact that Indians themselves were uninterested in learning these languages. As Duff demonstrated in his college in Calcutta and Macaulay noted in his Minute, the students had to be paid scholarships to motivate them to study Oriental literature, while they themselves were prepared to pay for an English education. The Orientalists had been a powerful enough influence in the Company to get their proposal approved to set up a new Sanskrit College in Calcutta in 1823. This move was the last straw, resulting in a strong reaction from enlightened Indian thinkers such as Raja Ram Mohun Roy, who denounced it as a step "best calculated to keep this country in darkness."

Another influential voice that opposed Oriental education was that of Bishop Heber of Calcutta, composer of the great hymn, "Holy, Holy, Holy. " He visited the Company-funded Benares Sanskrit College, and to his horror discovered that,

> "Under a grant ordered by Parliament on the pressure of the Christian public (of Britain), and administered by a Christian Government, a professor ... identified Mount Meroo with the

North Pole, declared that the tortoise of the Hindu cosmogony supported the earth from under the South Pole, pointed to Padalon in the centre of the globe, and demonstrated how the sun went round the earth every day and visited the signs of the Zodiac!"

In reaction to the above misuse of public funds for education, "Anglicists" such as Robert Mertins Bird, J. B. Colvin, and Charles Trevelyan, acting under Duff's influence, argued that in India's interest, the funds ought to be used for imparting a European education. They were not arguing for English language as the medium of education *per se*, but for a sharing of knowledge accumulated in England, in whatever medium was feasible. Macaulay opted for the English language as the temporary medium for what was then English or European education. He put it thus in the Minute itself:

> "We ought to employ them (our funds) in teaching what is best worth knowing; that English is better worth knowing than Sanskrit or Arabic; that the natives are desirous to be taught English, and are not desirous to be taught Sanskrit or Arabic;... that it is possible to make natives of this country thoroughly good English scholars, and that to this end our efforts ought to be directed....
>
> In one point I fully agree with the gentlemen to whose general views I am opposed. I feel, with them, that it is impossible for us, with our limited means, to attempt to educate the body of the people. We must do our best to form a class of persons, Indian in blood and colour, but English in taste, in opinions, in morals, and in intellect. To that class we may leave it to refine the vernacular dialects of the country, to enrich those dialects with terms of science borrowed from the Western nomenclature, and to render them, by degrees, fit vehicles for conveying knowledge to a great mass of the population."

It should be clear from the above that the long shadow of William Carey—the educationist and the great champion of the vernaculars—

was cast over this Minute. It became even clearer when Macaulay was asked if it was permissible to use the same public fund to teach "Hindee" at Ajmer. He wrote,

> "An order to give instruction in the English language is, by necessary implication, an order to give instruction, where that instruction is required, in the vernacular language. For what is meant by teaching a boy a foreign language? Surely this... teaching him what words in the foreign language correspond to certain words in his own vernacular language... enabling him to translate from the foreign language into his own vernacular language, and *vice versa*. We learn one language, our Mother Tongue, by noticing the correspondence between words and things. But all the languages, which we afterwards study, we learn by noticing the correspondence between the words in those languages and the words in our own Mother Tongue. The teaching the boys at Ajmer, therefore, to read and write Hindee seems to me to be *bona fide* a part of an English education."

THE REFORMS' GRAND FINALE

The dynamic faith of William Carey and Charles Grant in a sovereign and active God had led them to believe that God had given India to Britain, precisely for her salvation, not for her economic exploitation as a colony. Grant wrote in his book:

> "In considering the affairs of the world as under the control of the Supreme Disposer, and those distant territories... providentially put into our hands... is it not necessary to conclude that they are given to us, not merely that we might draw an annual profit from them, but that we might diffuse among their inhabitants, long sunk in darkness, vice and misery, the light and benign influence of the truth, the blessings of well-regulated society, the improvements and comforts of active industry?"

Grant had therefore gone on to argue in his book that the commercial interests of England would be better served by improving India, and not by enslaving it. That this viewpoint finally won the day was illustrated when, forty years later, in a speech in Parliament in 1833, Lord Macaulay—the son of Grant's friend Zachary Macaulay, a member of the evangelical "sect" of Clapham, a protege of Wilberforce, and the author of the Minute of 1835—expounded this thesis of Grant's book. In that historic speech Macaulay argued that England must pursue this policy of improving India, even if improvement meant India's eventual independence. For, "To trade with civilised men is infinitely more profitable than to govern savages." The following is a sample of the power of Macaulay's language and logic that overwhelmed the Parliament:

> "It may be that the public mind of India may expand under our system till it has outgrown that system; that by good Government we may educate our subjects into a capacity for better Government, that having become interested in European knowledge, they may in some future age, demand European institutions [of freedom]. Whether such a day will ever come I know not. But never will I attempt to avert or retard it. Whenever it comes it will be the proudest day in English history. To have found a great people sunk in the lowest depths of slavery and superstitions, to have so ruled them as to have made them desirous and capable of all the privileges of citizens, would indeed be a title to glory all our own. The sceptre may pass away from us. Unforeseen accidents may derange our most profound schemes of policy. Victory may be inconstant to our arms. But there are triumphs which are followed by no reverses. There is an empire exempt from all natural causes of decay. Those triumphs are the pacific triumphs of reason over barbarism; that empire is the imperishable empire of our arts and our morals, our literature and our laws."

The radical difference that a spiritual conversion made in these evangelical reformers is exemplified by their understanding of what the British conquest of India should mean. It is the very opposite of the typical British attitudes mentioned at the beginning of this chapter.

Charles Trevelyan, Macaulay's brother-in-law, summed up the long-term aim of the Christian reform movement, in 1838 in his pamphlet on *Education in India*. (Needless to say, Macaulay and Trevelyan, were articulating what Carey had already practiced and demonstrated.) Trevelyan wrote:

"The existing connexion between two such distant countries as England and India, cannot, in the nature of things, be permanent: No effort of policy can prevent the natives from ultimately regaining their independence. But there are two ways of arriving at this point. One of these is through the medium of revolution; the other through that of reform.... [Revolution] must end in the complete alienation of mind and separation of interests between ourselves and the natives; the other [reform] in a permanent alliance, founded on mutual benefit and good-will. The only means at our disposal for preventing [revolution] and securing... the results [of reform] is, to set the natives on a process of European improvement.... The natives will have independence, after first learning how to make good use of it; and we shall exchange profitable subjects for still more profitable allies.... Trained by us to happiness and independence, and endowed with our learning and political institutions, India will remain the proudest monument of British benevolence."

That anticipated day of India's independence and (evangelical) England's ultimate triumph finally came in 1947. Macaulay had anticipated it almost prophetically more than a century earlier. India asked for and became independent of the British Raj. Yet it retained and resolved to live by British laws and institutions as a member of the

British Commonwealth. For example, the Indian Penal Code of 1861, which is still the basis for law in Indian jurisprudence, was drafted by Macaulay himself as "Codes of Criminal and Civil Procedures," when he served as India's law minister.

Thus India's independence in 1947 was not only a victory for Mahatma Gandhi and the "freedom fighters," but even more fundamentally, a triumph for Carey's evangelical England. It marked the victory of the early missionaries over the narrow commercial, political, and military vested interests of England, as well as a victory for the heart and mind of India.

The violent movements and the human rights violations of the 1970s, 80s, and early 90s raise serious doubts about whether or not human rights and freedoms will last for long in India. They cannot last if India chooses to forget the faith and spirit of her modernisers.

Footnotes (Chapter 4)

---

[1] Ram Rajya is the mythical kingdom of the god-king Rama, where dharma or the Hindu idea of righteousness prevailed, and where each one performed the duties of their caste. The postmodern Hindu political party, the Bharatiya Janata Party, has been trying to turn India from a secular to a Hindu state, with the promise of establishing the Ram Rajya.

[2] The horrors of the Jaggannath festival (anglicized to Juggernaut) are vividly described by Buchanan in his Christian Researches in Asia (quoted by V. Mangalwadi in Missionary Conspiracy: Letters to a Postmodern Hindu). See the Note on page 114

Chapter Five

⊙⌘⌘⊙

THE MIND OF A MODERNISER

WHY WOULD WILLIAM CAREY OPPOSE *sati*, when he had himself observed that it was the widow's "voluntary choice" to be immolated on her husband's funeral pyre? Did he not believe in the right of the individual to make a free choice? Or, how could Carey assume that his efforts would help change a centuries-old religious-cultural tradition in Hindu India, administered by an irreligious British company that would not even permit a British missionary to reside in its territory?

This chapter is concerned with the question: Why did Carey attempt what he did? Why couldn't Indians or other British leaders have initiated what Carey ventured to do? And, for that matter, why don't Indian Christians today walk in Carey's footsteps, in this area of reform?

The central thesis of this chapter is that certain conscious or unconscious theological assumptions served as one of the basic dynamics behind William Carey's work. His knowledge of these truths came from his understanding of the Bible. Many segments of the Christian church today have ignored these basics of their doctrinal heritage. That is ironic because even the Hindu reformers of the nineteenth century had accepted at least some of these beliefs as being essential for their task of modernising India.

Without recovering these basics, we will succeed merely in a hollow "celebration" of the bicentenary of Carey's work in India. We could, no doubt, feel a second-hand or vicarious glory from his achievements; but if Carey is to become, not just a "hero," but a model who inspires radical discipleship, then it is imperative that his theological assumptions are understood and that they are taught from our pulpits.

The social climate of Carey's day and the historical factors that forged his mentality and his priorities were, obviously, significant. Nevertheless, his background and environment elicited a particular response from Carey because of his prior theological assumptions. While we cannot recreate history, there is nothing to prevent us from recovering the dynamics of Carey's theological assumptions—the mind of a moderniser.

The following aspects of Carey's worldview seem to be the most relevant for reform and modernisation. Most people never articulate the worldview which forms the intellectual grid through which they understand and respond to their environment. Therefore, it is not necessary to assume that Carey was always conscious of his theological reasons for reacting the way he did.

GOD AS THE CREATOR

The Doctrine of Creation and Science

Carey's deep and dogged interest in nature—in stones (geology), insects (biology), plants and flowers (botany and agriculture), trees (forestry), and the stars (astronomy)—was rooted in his understanding that this world was his Father's creation.

Obviously, the intellectual climate of England in which William Carey grew up was important in shaping his interest in studying natural science, publishing scientific books, and teaching science to his students. This scientific climate in England was a result of the biblical teaching that God had created the cosmos with His *Logos*. *Logos* is translated as "Word," "Wisdom," or "Reason." The Bible taught that human beings were created with minds similar to God's own rationality, so that we may understand the laws of nature and manage the earth. Carey was interested in the physical universe around him because he believed that our heavenly Father had blessed mankind both with the rationality to understand the creation and with the authority to govern it.

CREATION AND THE INDUCTIVE METHOD OF KNOWLEDGE

Even before Carey's time, the doctrine of creation as taught in Genesis 1 had already given birth to the inductive method of knowledge. Christian theological assumptions—that a) the universe is a stable system run by rational laws ordained by God, and that b) the universe is a book of God's "natural revelation" which can be and ought to be read by us, so that we may both c) learn about God's wisdom and power and also d) govern the earth—implied that objective knowledge was possible through careful observation.

Carey's *Enquiry* reflects a mind that investigates the facts. His entire appeal for world mission was based on meticulously collected data, not on an appeal to the emotions of the moment. One can say that the inductive method that John Calvin had applied to the Scriptures in his *Institutes*, and that served as the foundation for the scientific method articulated by Francis Bacon was, for the first time, applied by Carey to the field of missiology. The same methodology—finding objective facts (say, about *sati*) with the help of researchers—made Carey's writings powerful.

It should be obvious that this "religious" theory of how knowledge of truth (epistemology) is to be obtained, was the exact opposite of mystical, magical, and esoteric ideas of knowledge then prevalent in

India. Hindus did not translate their scriptures from Sanskrit into the languages of the people because the truth was not something to be understood rationally. It was to be experienced by "killing" the intellect through various means of meditation and yoga. In some religious traditions such as *Tantra*, a deliberately ambiguous and misleading language called *sandha-bhasha* was used, both to confuse and to discourage the non-initiate and also to remind the enlightened tantric that the reality he sought was beyond logical rationality. Even the non-tantric religions sought to annihilate meaningful/rational language through *mantras*. A *mantra* is a systematic annihilation of meaningful language by mechanical repetition of a word or sound. In Hinduism, the destruction of rationality was presumed to be a precondition for obtaining a knowledge of truth. Science, based on observation or inductive method, was thus ruled out a *priori* by India's religious tradition.

PHILOSOPHIES THAT UNDERMINE SCIENCE

The lack today of a similar interest in the natural sciences in the Indian church is rooted in a spirituality that sees God as Savior but fails to appreciate Him as Creator. Some versions of a new spiritual trend among Christians, known as "spiritual warfare," also accept, perhaps unconsciously, the essence of polytheism. They refuse to see that much of the occult phenomena is a hoax, not genuine instances of demons and demigods influencing material reality. In general, the spiritual warfare movement is right in rejecting a secularised, materialistic philosophy that ignores the supernatural. However, some versions of the movement undermine a basic feature of the biblical worldview, which is that the material realm is normally a stable order, open to scientific investigation, except when there is a miracle—an unusual supernatural intervention.[1]

The Hindu mindset at Carey's time did not acknowledge God as Creator. Either creation was considered to be a dream of God (*maya* or illusion), or worse still, creation itself was defined as divinity.

An implication of viewing creation as *maya* or illusion is to dislike it—to seek isolation or escape from it, not to love it and care for it.

The result of seeing the Creator and creation as one is to fall into the bondage of idolatry or mysticism. If creation is divine then we can fear it, worship it, absolutise it, or seek to become one with it, but we cannot assume the responsibility of understanding, managing, or changing it.

William Carey found India in the grip of chronic spiritual deprivation: In *folk* Hinduism, idolatry and polytheism (the worship of creation and gods and goddesses) had rendered the human mind incapable of governing creation and harnessing its potential for development; meanwhile, in *philosophic* Hinduism, mysticism had undercut the motivational and epistemological foundations of science.

Science and technology are a result of the human desire to enjoy nature by understanding it, subduing it, and establishing our rule over it. Science is based on the assumption that the universe has a stable, rational order. Polytheism and the occult, on the other hand, demolish the possibility of science by assuming that the natural universe is an unstable, magical system constantly changing according to the whims and fancies of supernatural beings. Mysticism can motivate us only to enjoy nature by feeling it in a non-rational way. Science has to be able to trust human rationality as a valid source of knowledge. Mysticism requires a systematic obliteration of rationality. Science has to insist on objectivity, even while recognising that we are subjects trying to be objective. Mysticism also precludes science because it begins when we cease being objective in our observation.

CREATION AND ECOLOGY

Today, there is a naive and mistaken notion in the West that our environmental crisis is a result of the human desire to have dominion over creation. The fact, on the contrary, is that we cannot manage the environment unless we see ourselves both as an integral *part* of creation, therefore dependent on it, but also as being *over* creation, and therefore being responsible for it. The environmental mess in India, which is far worse than in the industrialised West, is a clear indication that the worship of nature damages creation more than do our attempts to manage it. It is enough here to point out that it was William Carey and not the Hindu mystics who initiated the struggle for regenerating the eco-balance in India.

The Doctrine of Creation and Social Reform

Another implication of the belief that God is the Creator is that He is transcendent—apart from the physical and social realms, and above them. Our ability to change our physical, social, or political environment, as we shall see, is directly proportional to our ability to grasp both the significance of God's transcendence and authority over creation and our own God-given authority over creation.

This second ramification of the belief that God is the Creator also served as a decisive determinant in the modernisation of India. In this basic tenet, Carey found a moral basis for opposing evils such as *sati*. Many Indian reformers (e.g., Jotiba Phule) who succeeded Carey found this idea compelling. Today, ironically, the Western world, in a self-destructive mood, seems to be turning away from this second truth, namely, that, *if God is the author of a universe that exists objectively (independent from our experience of it) then reality—whether natural, social, or moral—has a given meaning and definition. This meaning is independent from how we perceive the universe around us.*

The significance of this principle for reform can be illustrated by Carey's battle against *sati*.

AN ILLUSTRATION

The culture of idol worship assumes that we are free to decide if a stone is a god or not. It implies that God has not given mankind a revelation of objective truth; therefore we can define reality ourselves and give to it whatever meaning we prefer. If this assumption is true, then a woman is free to imagine that her husband is her god and that she lives for him. Therefore, after he dies her own life has no meaning. This outrageous conclusion served as the hidden basis for a justification of *sati*.

For Carey, however, it was ultimately God who, as Creator, gave meaning and definition to His creation. God decides who we are, and what the true nature of the husband/wife relationship ought to be. Therefore, neither one's society nor any individual within that society is finally free to define himself and/or his relationships.

This belief meant that Carey had no problem in judging whether or not *sati* was evil. For him the relevant question was not whether or not *sati* was the voluntary act of a particular woman, or whether or not she was forced to kill herself. The objective fact, as far as Carey was concerned, was that a woman's life was neither her own nor her husband's. It was God's. And the Creator had not given us the right to violate His gift of life. Suicide is sin because it considers a life valueless which is, in fact, precious to the Creator; it sees a situation to be hopeless where God expects faith and patience.

CONTEMPORARY RELEVANCE

This theological factor was of enormous significance in a recent Indian debate on *sati*, which started with the Roop Kanwar episode in September 1987.[2] The following two factors make the danger of *sati's* revival a real possibility:

First, the democratic temper of our times suggests to many people that in the ultimate sense, the majority decides what is right or what is wrong. So, if the majority favors *sati*, it ought to be permitted.

The second factor is the current "New Age" belief that an individual is totally free to define his or her own reality. We indeed have freedom, but our freedom is limited because our freedom comes, not from being God, but from the fact (as we will consider later) that we are made in the image of God. We are not programmed machines, but persons with freedom of choice. We are therefore at liberty to have subjective/private perceptions of reality. This, too, has important implications for the process of modernisation: It sets us free to be creative.

However, since God is the Creator of the universe, including ourselves, reality already has an objective meaning given to it by Him. God's revelation sets limits to our freedom. We sin when we cross those limits. For example, a woman is free to see her husband as a lover or as an oppressor, as her master or as her partner. But she is not free to see him as her God. That, the Creator says, is idolatry and therefore sin.

It is possible to imagine that a group of Hindus could decide that a revival of *sati* would be a symbolic necessity for ridding India of its cultural colonisation by "Christian England." If a group decided to force a nationwide showdown on the issue (whether or not a Hindu woman is free to abide by her conscience to commit *sati*), then I have no doubt that the pro-*sati* lobby would win in India (just as the pro-abortion and pro-euthanasia lobbies have, for now, won in the West). I think the pro-*sati* lobby would win because the so-called "democratic" temper of our times and the modern idea of unbounded individual freedom favor their viewpoint.

The practice of *sati* does meet certain social needs, just as abortion, infanticide, and euthanasia do: The death of a high-caste man creates some peculiar socioeconomic problems, and by eliminating the widow, *sati* eliminates those problems. For example, if a widow remarries, does she take her husband's family property into another family or into another caste? If she could, then the poorer, lower-caste young men would love to marry the higher-caste widows!

The pro-*sati* lobby was defeated in the Privy Council in London in the early 1830s only because the British mind then shared Carey's theological assumption that the final source of law is the Law-giver, the Creator, not an individual nor the consensus of a society. We would have lived like amoral animals had not the Creator made us in His image, i.e., with the ability to make value judgments—both aesthetic and moral. In this sense, the law is what the Creator describes as the moral reality. Neither an individual nor the majority is free to violate the divinely-ordained moral categories.

Our generation is guided more by how we "feel about an issue," than by the facts of the situation. But am I to take care of creation because of how I feel about a particular issue or a particular species? Or am I to take care of it because I was created for that purpose? For the sake of the future of human civilisation, it is immensely important to recover, in our day, the truth that an objective physical and moral universe exists (independently of our perception); that God is its Author; that He, ultimately, defines it and gives it value and meaning; and that we have to abide by His Word irrespective of how we feel.

HUMAN BEINGS AS GOD'S IMAGE

A moderniser has simultaneously to hold on to two elementary beliefs: first, that a given physical-moral reality exists independently of his perception of it; and second, that he has the ability to alter that reality. That may sound obvious today. When Carey arrived in India, he found a civilisation that had deliberately denied both of these essential beliefs and consequently was powerless to improve.

Both of these ideas, however, were part of William Carey's mindset. On the one hand the Bible affirmed that the objective universe had a definition and meaning given by the Creator Himself. Yet, on the other hand, the same Bible also liberated post-Reformation Europe to imagine and create a world better than that which it experienced. This freedom to be imaginative and creative was fundamental to the reforms and developments of the centuries immediately preceding Carey.

Let us first consider an obvious implication of the doctrine that human beings are made in God's image, after which we can look at other implications that are not so obvious in our day.

Human Life Is Precious

It should not require much imagination to see that Carey's struggle to save the lives of innocent infants—the potential victims of infanticide; widows—the potential victims of *sati*; and lepers—the potential victims of our cultural beastliness, was rooted in his understanding that human life is precious because men and women are neither machines, nor animals, but persons created in God's image. The Bible prohibited murder precisely on this premise.

What may not be quite so obvious is that many Christians today fail to stand up in defence of human life, because they think that only the human *soul*—and, not the human body as well—reflects God's image.

By *imago Dei*, or the "image of God," the Bible, of course, does not mean that God has a physical form such as our own. It does mean that when God breathed into Adam and he became a "living soul"-a unity of body and spirit—Adam began to share, in a finite way, some of God's attributes, such as self-awareness, rational intelligence, volition, verbal communication, creativity, the ability to make value judgments, and the ability to rule over creation (i.e., to impose on the external environment the results of his intellect, will, and verdicts). A human being, even though a sinner, is precious because he is the crown of God's creativity on this earth.

The Hindu mind that Carey encountered had no such philosophic basis for fighting either to preserve human life or to affirm its dignity. On the contrary, it pictured human life as being in bondage to the wheel of *samsara*. Individuality, according to Hinduism, was at best suffering, and at worst a hideous illusion. Almost the entire mainstream Indian orientation had been a negation of life. When it did affirm life, such as in the Tantric tradition, it tended to exalt the sordid. The process of modernisation had to begin with someone who was committed to the biblical view that even the life of a leper or a cobbler is precious and that every human being has to be transformed until he or she fully reflects God's glory.

We Share Something of God's Transcendence Over Nature

The Oxford English Dictionary defines God's transcendence as "existing apart from, not subject to limitations of, the material universe." A disembodied spirit exists apart from and without some of the limitations of physical laws such as gravity.

Our physical bodies are a part of the material universe and are therefore subject to its limitations. ("Dust thou art, and unto dust shalt thou return.") But being made in God's image means that, even as physical beings we can transcend some of the limitations of nature and alter physical reality. For example, in a dark room animals are limited by their ability (or lack of ability) to see in the dark, but we humans are not bound by such limits—we can turn on a light. Similarly, when traveling through a desert we can bring water along with us. We are not completely limited by external reality. God has made us creative. We are free to imagine a different and better physical, social, and political world. Where there is oppression, we can dream of freedom and dignity for the smallest individual.

WE TRANSCEND REALITY IN OUR IMAGINATION AND ARTS

Carey is a classic example of Christian thinking not ruled by fatalistic resignation. Rather than resigning ourselves to a wrong or unacceptable situation, we should use our creative imagination to make a difference. Being made in God's image has ramifications both for scientific innovations and for social reform. God saw physical darkness and, as we read in Genesis, He proceeded to create light. Later, in the gospels, we read that He saw our moral-social darkness and sent Jesus to be the Light of life. As God's children, we too have to transcend the natural/ social scene around us and make a difference. Jesus said to His disciples, "You are the light of the world."

William Carey was not surprised by the moral and social darkness he saw in India, nor did he accept it as final or unchangeable. He knew that he had been sent to India to be light, and he sought to make a difference in his surroundings. It cannot be denied that today the Indian mood, including the mood of Indian Christians, is pessimistic. Many think that the social evils of caste and political corruption in India are the given facts of life—beyond transformation. This mentality results from a lack of understanding that we are created qualitatively different so that we can make a difference in our environment.

Creativity and imagination are often expressed first of all in arts and literature. For example, Europe experienced the darkness of the holocaust in the 1940s, and it produced powerful works of art about that dark period. Those literary and artistic works have had such a profound impact on the present generation that it is difficult to imagine similar state-sponsored brutalities ever being repeated there. During the partition of India and Pakistan in 1947, the Indian subcontinent went through its own version of a "holocaust"—a massacre of Hindus, Sikhs, and Muslims by each other. Yet no comparable works of imagination and creativity were created to lament and counter that darkness.

The result is that even today the Indian mind is not ashamed of communal killings. They have become a regular feature of social life, blatantly encouraged by "religious" and political leaders! Indians have resigned themselves to live with the darkness of communal clashes.

William Carey used his imagination in the literary arena to make a difference in his social environment. Carey wrote his *Colloquies*—"a lively depiction of manners and notions of the people of Bengal"—as a contribution to Bengali literature. He encouraged and published both comical and literary books such as *Tota Itihas*—"Parrot's History"!

Where Carey saw barren wilderness, he did not revert to lamenting but began to plan forests. He studied trees, planted them, and then taught forestry. Where he saw weeds, he imagined gardens, cultivated them, published books, and established forums such as the Agri-Horticultural Society of India to help give sustained support to his initiatives.

Undoubtedly the spiritual bankruptcy of many Christians in our time is closely related to the bankruptcy of godly imagination. True, many Christians do seek to be transformed into the *moral* image of God, but there is little desire among Indian Christians to exercise the *creative* dimension in them of the Maker's image. Many church leaders and their congregations in India do not plan worship services creatively, let alone plan for the landscaping of their church compounds or the surrounding countryside. (Many Hindu pilgrim centers, despite being wealthier than Christian churches, are aesthetically even worse. They offer a study in contrast between God-made beauty and religion-inspired ugliness.)

WE TRANSCEND REALITY THROUGH WORK

In Carey's mind imagination itself was not reality. Today, "creative visualisation" has become very popular in the treatment of various illnesses. Some physical illnesses that are rooted in our own choices and feelings can indeed be cured by this practice because the mind does transcend matter. However, it is foolish to think that all reality is in the mind and to look upon meditation as a panacea for our ecological and other external problems.

Carey knew that the cosmos is a result not only of God's thoughts but also of His work. We too are created to work hard to establish our rule on earth. Carey was not simply an imaginative person; he saw himself primarily as a worker. And for him, "work" was not merely a job or a career, but a means of establishing human dominion over the material realm ... a means of partially realising God's image in ourselves.

The evangelicals of Carey's generation were convinced that we become less of God's image when we choose to be lazy. Many of them religiously wrote their daily journals and, if they thought that they had wasted time on a particular day they repented. Wasting time and not being diligent in work, were serious moral issues for them. This attitude, a key factor behind the modernisation of Europe, has been called the "Protestant work ethic." It helped Protestant Europe to march ahead of non-Protestant Europe.

Carey injected this work ethic into Indian society. Hindu spirituality had taken the best of India's children away from work, into *ashrams*—which etymologically means *a* (non) *shram* (labour). To be spiritual in India implied the very opposite of what Carey understood it to mean: In India to be spiritual meant to meditate, not labour. When the divinity is seen as an impersonal consciousness or energy, and man is assumed to be divine, then spirituality is automatically seen as an attempt to depersonalise ourselves. Hindu religious discipline, therefore, was an attempt to annihilate rationality through mysticism, language through *mantra*, creative imagination through *yoga* or systematic emptying of the mind, and work through meditation and the *ashram* system. In this milieu, Carey's religious ethic of work was a revolution.

WE ARE MEANT TO HAVE DOMINION OVER TIME

Should our times be governed by our "stars," through astrologers, or are we created to plan and manage our time? In other words, are we created in the image of our stars, or in the image of God who created the "stars" and rules over them? These are not theoretical issues. A society that answers to them substantially determines whether it will advance or remain static and underdeveloped. By introducing the study of astronomy into the classroom, Carey brought the modernising idea that space and time were a part of the physical world we were made to govern. The Hindu ideas of four *yugas* (periods in a cosmic cycle) and reincarnation, as well as the all-pervasive faith in astrology, had conspired to relegate individuality to a transient phenomenon in time. If our times are ruled by our stars, then we cannot plan or manage our days and hours in terms of our own goals. We have to wait for the set "auspicious moments."

Carey's interest in astronomy came from the fact that, with the help of the stars, sailors such as Captain Cook had opened the sea routes for European trade with the Far East. Carey felt that Christians ought to use these routes for missions. But there was also a more basic theological dimension to his interest in astronomy. Various means of divination, including astrology, had enslaved the human spirit in India with chains of fear and superstition, making it vulnerable to exploitation by unscrupulous priests and astrologers. This made biblical injunctions against divination come alive in Carey's mind, reassuring him that God's Word was the light that India needed for her emancipation.

The Bible teaches (in Genesis 1:14–18) that the sun and the moon are not deities, but objects created to govern the day and night. Along with the other heavenly bodies, they were created also as "signs," or "markers" for giving us a sense of direction as well as a sense of history— for days and years, and seasons. Human beings, created to "subdue the earth and have dominion over it," could study geography and history, and thus could govern, because of the reference points provided by these heavenly bodies. Putting it differently: If the heavenly bodies were not there, or were invisible, we could not know north from south, or day from night, let alone make calendars. According to the Bible, the sun and the moon, as markers, divide time for us into small and manageable parts, so that we can plan our work and obey God's command to work for six days and rest on the seventh. Without markers by which to divide our time, we would invariably carry over one week's work into the next. We would not be able to plan, manage, or govern.

India's backwardness is substantially rooted in the false view of time propagated by her religious teachers. Development requires a correct understanding of human destiny in relation to the universe of space and time. Human beings are above time, firstly, by virtue of the fact that we share the image of God, who is above the universe of space and time; and secondly, because we were made to live "forever." Our individuality is not a passing phenomenon that will be reincarnated as something else the next time around. Adam, as Adam, was created to live forever. That changed after sin entered the scene. One of sin's consequences was death. Death has put human beings "under time"; we die, while time appears to go on and on. Carey came to preach the Good News of Jesus Christ, which says that human beings can once again have "eternal life." When Jesus died on the cross, He took our sins and its result—death—upon Himself. When He rose again from the dead, He defeated death—our final enemy. The New Testament teaches that Christ's resurrection has colossal consequences for us. The resurrected Jesus said, "I am... the Beginning and the End" (Revelation 21:6). If we are in Him, we will also reign with Him forever. "Forever" means that we are not under time, but above it. While, as created beings, we will always remain finite, we can still have the authority to plan and manage the course of our days and years, just as we can also regulate the course of a river or plan the crops of a field. By resisting the superstitions of

Indian culture, such as faith in astrology, palmistry, and other forms of divination; and by teaching about the Resurrection—God's triumph over death in history—Carey was setting India free from an enslaving concept of time; he was modernising the Indian mind at a very fundamental level.

WE SHARE GOD'S TRANSCENDENCE OVER "PRINCIPALITIES AND POWERS"

For Carey's contemporaries, one of the biggest deterrents to the mission was the oppressive socio–political power structures of the "heathen" countries such as India. Having grown up in "civilised" societies, they could not consider living in countries governed by the "laws of the jungle." Carey confronted this objection head-on in his *Enquiry*:

"As to their uncivilised, and barbarous way of living, this can be no objection (to mission)... It was no objection to the apostles and their successors, who went among the barbarous Germans and Gauls, and still more barbarous Britons! They did not wait for the ancient inhabitants of these countries to be civilised before they could be Christianised, but went simply with the doctrine of the Cross; and Tertullian could boast that "those parts of Britain which were proof against the Roman armies, were conquered by the Gospel of Christ"—it was no objection to an Elliot, or a Brainerd, in later times. They went forth, and encountered every difficulty of the kind, and found that a cordial reception of the Gospel produced those happy effects which the longest intercourse with Europeans, without it, could never accomplish... After all, the uncivilised state of the heathen, instead of affording an objection *against* preaching the Gospel to them, ought to furnish an argument *for* it... Can we hear that they are without the Gospel, without Government, without laws, and without arts, and sciences, and not exert ourselves to introduce amongst them the sentiments of men, and of Christians? Would not the spread of the Gospel be the most effectual means of their civilisation? Would not that make them useful members of society?"

Carey expressed similar thoughts in the introduction to his *Enquiry*:

"As our blessed Lord has required us to pray that His kingdom may come, and His will be done on earth as it is in heaven, it becomes us not only to express our desires of that event by words, but to use every lawful method to spread the knowledge of His name... Sin was introduced amongst the children of men by the fall of Adam, and has ever since been spreading... Yet God repeatedly made known His intention to prevail finally over all the power of the Devil, and to destroy all his works, and set up His own kingdom and interest among men, and extend it as universally as Satan had extended his. It was for this purpose that the Messiah came and died, that God might be just and the justifier of all that should believe in Him. When He had laid down His life, and taken it up again, He sent forth His disciples to preach the good tidings to every creature, and to endeavour by all possible methods to bring over a lost world to God."

What made Carey so confident that the oppressive social and political structures of this world could be reformed? One cause was the obvious cultural impact of the Wesleyan revivals, already becoming apparent in his own generation. But a more important reason was his understanding that the Lord Himself had promised that darkness would not overcome the light and that the Gospel was like the small amount of leaven, put into a batch of flour, that gradually transformed the whole dough.

It should be clear from the above quotations that Carey was a moderniser chiefly because his mind was motivated by a theological optimism: Satan's kingdom had already been defeated in history, by the death and resurrection of Jesus; Christ was already King over all the kings of this world; believers were already seated with Christ who, in turn, was above all powers and principalities of this dark age. Therefore, Carey understood that Christ's command to, "Make disciples of all nations... teaching them to obey everything I have commanded you" (Matthew 28:19–20) implied that the nations *could* be discipled before Christ's return.

The tragedy of our times is that, while many Christians have confidence in the power of the Lord to return and change the world, many of us do not have confidence in the power of the Gospel to transform society now. Carey struggled against specific social evils, just as his friends in England were continuing their struggle against specific evils. But Carey's confidence was not in his social protest or social action, but in the Gospel. This is the very opposite of those Christians today who put their hope for change in their "social action." It is also different from the faith of those who believe that the world can improve only after Christ returns. Carey became a reformer because he understood the breadth of the theological concept of the "kingdom of God." He believed that if we disciple nations, we will increasingly see God's will being done here on earth.

Lord Wellesley and William Carey were deeply aware of the immorality among the young men, aged fifteen to twenty years, who were arriving from England to administer India. Carey believed that he could influence the political administration of India, since Jesus Christ was above the powers and principalities of the world, and Carey himself was His servant. Therefore, besides teaching languages to these newly arrived administrators, Carey strove for three decades to shape their moral character as well. As a missionary, his priorities were naturally opposite to those of the Company's servants, who had come to India to create wealth for themselves and their nation. His compassion for the needs of India, together with his gentleness, were a great influence on his British pupils.[3]

Even the most skeptical of the Indian historians have to admit that, during Carey's tenure as a teacher, the character of the civil servant trainees underwent a radical transformation. India became a showpiece of colonial administration, better governed than the colonies of Germany, France, Holland, and Denmark. There can be no doubt that the continuing decline in the moral and professional standards in the Indian civil service today is an indication of the deliberate rejection of Carey's heritage.

Our call, however, is not to succumb to resignation and mourning for what is lost. We are called to summon the nation to repentance and to suffering for righteousness. The nation has lost its standards because the church has forgotten the truth that it is seated with Christ above all the principalities and powers of this dark age. It is sad that those Christians who talk the most about "spiritual warfare" against the principalities and powers, seem to understand it the least. Today they tend to see themselves primarily as a "minority besieged by satanic principalities and powers." They don't seem to realise that they are servants of the One who claimed, "All power is given unto me in heaven and in earth" (Matthew 28:18, KJV). Some Christians in India are so paralysed by a minority complex that they keep casting demons from, say, broken-down refrigerators, but they never, lamentably, become a reforming force.

All People Can Change, Because We Are All Made in God's Image

For Carey, another implication of the fact that we are made in God's image was that even the most wretched of this world, the "scum of the earth," can be transformed. Carey was well aware of the depravity in the countries where he wanted to see missions become active. Yet, he wrote in his *Enquiry*:

"Barbarous as these poor heathens are, they appear to be as capable of knowledge as we are; and in many places, at least, have discovered uncommon genius and tractableness."

Carey himself had humble origins. As a shoemaker in England, he had found that God's grace was sufficient for him. He rejected the British class system and actively opposed the racism inherent in the slave trade, refusing to buy goods made by slave labour. It follows that it was not possible for him to condone the caste system in India.

Carey understood that his open social interaction with untouchables would, at least initially, slow the rate of conversions. Yet he chose not to compromise with caste distinctions—a fundamental evil of Indian society. His mission was not to collect a large number of "converts" but to see God's overall will be done in individual lives and the culture of India. Carey knew that, ultimately, his commitment to truth alone would be fruitful. After a low-caste person was baptised, he would celebrate by sitting and eating with the converts from all castes and with Europeans, the colonial rulers—a revolutionary gesture at that time. Even today, sadly, such behaviour is radical in India's caste-ridden society. From virtually every part of India, we still hear stories of Christian leaders refusing to accept low-caste people into church membership because they allegedly "lower the cultural, intellectual, and even moral standing of the church."

This attitude, among other factors, is undoubtedly a result of a lack of confidence in the power of the Gospel to restore God's image to the lowly. Carey remained committed to the downtrodden till the end of his life because he believed that every human being could choose to become a child of God.

GOD CALLS INDIVIDUALS

Initially, Fort William College refused to appoint Carey as a full professor, because he was not an Anglican. Instead, he was offered a tutorship earning only Rs. 500 instead of Rs. 1,500. For most of us today, it is incomprehensible that out of this salary, Carey would keep only Rs. 40 as pocket money for himself, and give the balance to his mission.

Obviously, to understand Carey we need to understand Carey's view of vocation, an important concept of Protestant Christianity during his time.

Vocation and Work

The idea of vocation is illustrated by the apostle Paul. When Paul had his conversion experience on the road to Damascus, he was "called" to be an apostle to the Gentiles. It was an honour to be called personally by the Lord of the Universe to do something special for him. Therefore, Paul—a thinker and a teacher—was willing to stitch tents, on occasion, so that he might have the economic resources to fulfil his "calling" or vocation.

The Puritan theologian William Perkins (1558–1602), in his *Treatise on Calling* (published nearly two centuries before Carey), taught that as soon as a person becomes a Christian he or she should be taught to wait upon the Lord in order to find a calling. Today we do teach about prayer, Bible study, evangelism, and social work, but not about that most personal meeting with God. At best, our "work" is understood as our "vocation." Our work can also be our vocation, but it is not always so. Carey's calling was not to work in an indigo factory, but he was prepared to take up such work for the sake of his vocation. Unlike Carey, our young people will continue to seek the best paid, most secure, and the least demanding jobs as long as work is understood in secular terms—as a job (making money), or as a career (pursuing power, prestige, and influence)—and work is automatically baptised "vocation." Truly, however, a missionary is a "called one" who waits on the Lord to be commissioned by Him. A missionary is thus a reformer because he is a person of destiny.

Vocation and Destiny

Hinduism could not produce a person such as Carey, because the idea of individual destiny is alien to Hindu culture, which emphasises the dissolution of one's individuality, not its fulfillment. In fact, most people who speak Hindi, my mother tongue, would not even know that a Hindi equivalent for the word *destiny* (*niyati*) exists in dictionaries. (I have never read or heard the word, only seen it in the dictionary.) The word commonly used, and the idea that dominates Hindi literature, is *fate*—the exact opposite of the Christian concept of destiny.

It is a serious matter that the Western cinema, for example, seems more interested today in glamorising the very ideas that destroyed Indian civilisation—the concepts of *karma* and fate. If one were to judge contemporary Western civilisation by its entertainment media, it would seem that the notion of destiny—the force that propelled men such as William Carey to heroic and altruistic service—has now been lost.

The industry and staying power of a William Carey cannot be recovered by the Indian church unless our pulpits recover the lost doctrine of vocation unless we experience the reality that God wants to enter into a personal and direct working partnership with individuals who have become His children. Everyone wants a nine-to-five job. Carey had a five-to-ten—job-5:00 A.M. to 10:00 or 11:00 P.M.! He persevered because he had received his work assignment from God Himself.

Vocation and Individualism

Carey's heroism—a result of his understanding of vocation and destiny—represents the best form of the Western individualism that followed the Protestant Reformation. One central emphasis of the Gospel is that each individual has to stand alone before God and give an account of his life. I cannot blame others for my life, any more than Adam could blame Eve for eating the forbidden fruit. I am responsible for my choices. I have to trust God and obey Him, whether or not those close to me obey Him. If I have disobeyed, I have sinned and I need to repent.

Christian life begins with repentance that leads to conversion. Repentance implies a radical individualism—a person assuming responsibility for his or her life. In India, religion had been a tool of social control over a person's conscience, an instrument for quashing a person's individuality. In contrast, when Jesus called His disciples to "forsake all" for the kingdom of God, He set them free to be themselves, to follow God and fulfil their destiny—their calling. Christ's disciples, as a result, became heroes who turned the world upside down. Sixteenth-century Reformers and nineteenth-century missionaries who followed Carey's initiative resembled Christ's apostles at this point.

We should be grateful that some parts of the Indian church today have recaptured Carey's missionary vision and the individual heroism that accompanies it. They are the best hope for India's marginalised millions.

These remarks are not to imply that all facets of Western individualism are good or are rooted in biblical teaching. One stream of individualism that sprang from Enlightenment thinking was the kind summed up in the ethic of "self-reliance" taught by Emerson. This increasingly dominant form of individualism turns individual self-reliance into selfishness. Carey's individualism, like his Lord's, was both self-sacrificing and balanced by the biblical emphasis on the church being a body.

THE CHURCH AS A BODY

The Serampore trio—Carey, Marshman, and Ward—generated immense power for bringing about spiritual, intellectual, and social change in India because they believed that they were called to be a "body." They sought to obey this call by living as a community-sharing a common purse and a common mission.

The church is not meant to be a collection of heroes but a community knit together by love—a fruit of the Holy Spirit. If Carey had failed at this point he would have been forgotten a long time ago. He was the leader. He stood tall above the others, but without their support, his endeavors would have amounted to little. He needed them for even such basic requirements as looking after his own children, because of Dorothy's mental illness.

Hinduism as a religion had divided people into castes. This was a primary source of India's weakness. Foreign invaders were able to come to India with small armies and conquer and rule a large populace by exploiting the divisions inherent in the caste system. Carey wanted to strengthen India by uniting people across caste barriers. He knew that, through the Gospel, God Himself was uniting people into one body.

The church was inaugurated, supernaturally, on the day of Pentecost (Acts 2). On that day the Holy Spirit had given the disciples the ability to speak the languages of all the nations from where the devout had gathered in Jerusalem for the festival. That event was the great reversal of the incident in Genesis 11, when, supernaturally, mankind was divided (as a punishment) into different language groups. The plot of the book of Acts centers around God's uniting the Aramaic-speaking Jewish believers with those who spoke Greek, then uniting both of these groups with the "untouchable" half-Jewish Samaritans, and then uniting all of these Jewish believers with the hated Gentiles. The Jews did not allow men and women to worship together; the Gospel made them one. It also united the slaves with the free men into one body.

This understanding that through the church God was creating a new race, a body for Himself, naturally forced Carey to try to reform the very structure of Indian society. He resolved that caste would be broken in his church; that all who become God's children by faith in Christ must become equal members of God's household.

The schools and the college at Serampore taught children of all castes in the vernacular, in an attempt to break down caste. In contrast, many English-medium schools and colleges started and run by Christians who followed Carey, catered mainly to high-caste Hindus— as a matter of policy and convenience! This had tragic consequences. Christian education was gradually swallowed up by the very evil it was seeking to eradicate. The seats in these institutions were filled by the high-caste students who later, as graduates retaining their caste prejudices, became the teachers. This prepared an English-speaking casteist elite to recapture the whole nation when the British were ready to pack up and leave. This elite considered themselves "modern" because they spoke English rather than Sanskrit. But for all practical purposes, their medieval mentality has continued to this day. It weakens India by permitting an elitist language to be a barrier that divides Indians from each other.

Thus the Christian English-medium education, tragically, became the chief means of undermining India's modernisation, of handing India back to the slavery of Brahmanism. Low-caste social reformers such as Mahatma Jotiba Phule of Pune saw the disastrous consequence of this compromise with the evil of caste. Phule's followers, such as Dr. Bhimrao Ambedkar, rightly saw that an emasculated Christianity had ceased to be of much value to the downtrodden in India. Therefore, he chose instead to try Buddhism as a possible hope for those yearning to be freed from the slavery of caste.

THE GOSPEL AS THE POWER OF GOD FOR TOTAL SALVATION

Conservative Christians have admired William Carey because he reawakened the church to its commission to evangelise the world. Theologically liberal Christians have admired him because he triggered India's social reform movement. Historians, both Christians such as G.

A. Oddie and non-Christians such as Sen Gupta, have misunderstood Carey's social action as being incidental to his passion to "save souls."

The truth, however, is clear from his *Enquiry*: Even before coming to India, in 1792, in the middle of the French Revolution's 'Reign of Terror', Carey had understood that the Gospel had liberated parts of Europe from the "Dark Ages." He was convinced that the Gospel can also dispel India's socio-spiritual darkness. This deep conviction sustained Carey's chief labour: to make the Bible available to the Indian masses in their own languages.

It is worth repeating: Our mistake today is that some who believe the Gospel look upon it merely as a means of private salvation, for going to heaven. They do not seem to realise that the Gospel is the God-given "public truth"—the means of organising a decent society. Therefore, their faith becomes privately engaging but publicly irrelevant. On the other hand, those "Christian" activists who do not believe the basic truth of the Gospel, that Jesus Christ died and rose again for our sin, attach themselves to ideologies that are most popular in their day. For example, some of my friends, until recently, prided themselves on being Christian-Marxists or Socialists. In contrast to both the conservatives and the liberals, William Carey knew that Jesus is the "Light of the world"—not just the One who lights the way to heaven. Carey sought to reflect that Light in the world because he believed that the Church, as the body of Christ, was created to shine His light in a dark world.

Unfortunately, many Christians today who are sincerely trying to serve society, are oblivious to the power that God has already given to us—His light to dispel darkness. They tend to put their hope for social change primarily in their own projects. Thus, it appears that their main anxiety is how to keep getting financial aid for their particular programs. I know of many projects in India that survive only because the project holders are willing to bribe officials, thus participating in one of the main evils of Indian society today.

Why have we sunk to this level? I suggest that one factor is the materialistic presupposition of our age. Since the time of Karl Marx many have assumed, often unconsciously, that material reality is basic and that the moral/intellectual/spiritual aspects of reality are secondary—that they are mere by-products of economic reality. Carey, on the other hand, believed that the real battle is in the mind. False beliefs lead to wrong behaviour and harmful culture. Therefore, Carey strove to fill the Indian mind with the truth of God's Word. That, he understood, was conversion—the cornerstone in the task of civilising. God's mission, that Carey sought to fulfill, was to fill the earth with the knowledge of God as the waters cover the sea. (Isaiah 11:9).

CONCLUSION

In *A New History of Methodism*, W. J. Townsend writes,

> "Important eras of human progress and national salvation are generally inaugurated and moulded by a man who has understanding of the times, whose ear is open and attuned to respond sympathetically to the sighs and groans of humanity for redemption from the powers of evil, and who has the constructiveness and comprehensiveness of nature to become a builder of a nation and a hero of far reaching reformation."

AH. Oussoren adds,

> "These words may be applied to William Carey. Just like all great leaders of humanity, he not only understood his own time, but also had a clear conception of the times before him. He saw their corruption, their baseness, their frivolity, their deplorable state of affairs everyday."

But unlike most of us, Carey never gave up hope for India, because he looked beyond man, beyond society, to God's saving act in human history. Carey put his confidence for our salvation in the power of the

Gospel; that is, in the power of the death and resurrection of Jesus Christ to deliver us from our sin.

Footnotes (Chapter 5)

---

[1] The concept of a war between good and evil in the supernatural realm is biblical. However, the terminology of "spiritual warfare" as it is often used by unthinking Christians becomes unbiblical because it seems to deny God's sovereignty. It suggests that not God but territorial spirits rule the world. That seems to reinforce Hindu polytheism and New Age spiritism. Man was created to have dominion over the planet. Therefore, he has to assume the responsibility for what goes wrong. Passing the buck onto spirit entities undermines the significance of human choices. That is already problematic in India. "Spiritual warfare" terminology such as "conquering enemy territory" when unexplained, inflames some Hindus. They misinterpret it and make it a convenient justification for persecuting evangelists. "It is the missionary movement," they say, "which has declared a war on India."

[2] Roop Kanwar, an eighteen-year-old upper-caste widow, committed sati in 1987 in a village in Rajasthan. The national press in India reported it as a three-line news item on a back page. Thirteen days later I followed up with a front page piece for the Indian Express-and it became a major national controversy. Such coverage put Hindu women's rights on the national agenda for the first time since our independence in 1947. At the end of 1996 the court acquitted Roop Kanwar's relatives of the charges of abetting sati. The press has been filled with stories of how sati is currently being glorified in the state of Rajasthan; millions throng to the temples dedicated to women who have committed sati. Their pictures are used on things such as greeting cards.

[3] Both Fort William College in Calcutta and Haileybury College in England, where civil servants were trained to administer India, were run largely by evangelical missionaries and clergy.

Chapter Six

❦

WHY DO THEY HATE WILIAM CAREY?

"William Carey was the nastiest Englishman that ever came to India," asserted Mr. R. M. Pandit, my fellow passenger en route to London. He was going there to research Carey in connection with his 250th anniversary on 17 August 2011.

Panditji's confident manner encouraged me to ask:

Who was Carey? How was he nasty to us?

"In England, he was just a chamar—a low-class cobbler. In 1793, he violated the British Parliament's ban on missionary activity in India and slipped in as an undercover Baptist missionary. He started the chain reaction that culminated in our day, a chamar woman becoming the ruler of UP - the very heartland of Hinduism."

Why should that be so worrying? I wondered out loud. *After all, UP's Chief Minister, Ms. Mayawati is dependent on Brahmins and they can easily ditch her in the next election.*

"I'm not concerned about one Mayawati," clarified Panditji. "My concern is that Carey brought to India certain cancer cells that have continued to multiply. They are infecting Hindu parties such as the BJP. Why do you think the BJP routinely appoints Shudras as chief minister in the states it rules: Why can't it respect Hindu culture and promote professional rulers?"

I'm sorry Panditji, I said sheepishly, *but I've no idea what you are talking about. If Carey was born two hundred and fifty years ago, how is he responsible for what the BJP does today? If he was really the worst Englishman, why don't we hear more about him?*

Panditji became eager to educate me: "Other Europeans came to colonise and loot India militarily, politically, and economically but William Carey came to change India. He pioneered the missionary movement with a goal to colonise our minds, harvest our souls, and destroy our culture. This is the worst kind of colonialism."

I'm afraid Sir, you have to explain to me how one colonises the mind, I requested the scholar.

"Why do you think that a low-caste Shudra in Tamil Nadu and a Dalit in Bihar designate themselves as 'Dravidians'? Their forefathers saw themselves as an intrinsic part of the Aryan culture. Who changed our language of *Varna* into that of distinct races—Aryans and Dravidians?

Before Carey, some European scholars had taken an interest in Indian languages and literature. But Carey turned that academic curiosity into missionary mischief. He inspired other missionary-linguists to build on these foundations, diminishing Sanskrit's cultural prominence."

I've never heard this before, I assured Panditji. My inquisitiveness encouraged him to explain:

"Hindu sages engineered a harmonious society. *Varna* and *Jati* that the British mistranslated as Caste categorised us along a family's expertise. It allowed parents to teach their children how to excel in their family's profession. How can someone who milks cows teach his son to govern a state or navigate the sea? You tell me, do all human beings appear equal to you? Did the white Christians in America treat their black slaves as equal?"

Definitely not, I said, but Mahatma Phule was a contemporary of Abraham Lincoln and he praised devout Christians for fighting against their fellow whites to emancipate black slaves. That is why the blacks in America love the Bible even more than the white people do. Didn't President Obama put his hand on Lincoln's Bible to take his oath of office?

"The story that God made all human beings male and female - equally in his image does come from the Bible. But educated people believe in Evolution. Of course, no one has actually seen a fish evolve into a bird, but Evolution confirms what our sages taught us that some people are more evolved than others. How can everyone evolve equally? Evolution presupposes the fact of inequality but because Carey was a chamar, he wanted us to believe the Bible's myth of human equality. He converted ignorant people and required them to break caste by eating together."

What strategies did he use to change India?

"One was to propagate the myth that men and women were created equal: his mission started educating girls as well as boys."

What's wrong with that?

"You only change what you don't like. In order to change India, Carey had to misrepresent our culture."

In what ways?

"He published papers against the nobility of upper-caste women who committed sati by climbing onto the funeral pyres of their deceased husbands to join them in the afterlife. His paper launched the campaign that enabled the British government to abolish the sacred tradition of sati."

Really? I always heard that it was Raja Ram Mohan Roy who stopped widow burning.

"Roy was Carey's disciple. A Sanskrit scholar, Hariharananda Vidyabagish took Ram Mohan Roy to William Carey to learn English. The three of them fabricated *Maha Nirvana Tantra* (The Book of the Great Liberation). It pretended to codify ancient Sanskrit law, proving that the Hindu scriptures did not command a widow to commit sati."

"For decades the British courts yielded to the authority of this book in interpreting Hindu law. Using that spurious book in law, courts made Roy and the Tagore clan wealthy. Roy parted company with Carey and his mission because he became a Unitarian Christian. But throughout his life, he advanced Carey's agenda to destroy our ancient culture. Along with the missionaries, he became the primary reason why Macaulay ruled that the Company's money should be used to teach English, not Sanskrit. Colonial rulers wanted to inject English ideas into Indian vernaculars and Roy defended that."

"Roy followed Carey in condemning the very core of Hinduism—worship of idols and nature. He smuggled Christianity into Bengal, disguising it as Brahmo Samaj. His college was a platform for missionaries such as Alexander Duff."

Trying to make sense of what I was hearing, I asked: *What exactly did Carey do to corrupt India?*

Answering at a popular level: "Why is Hindi our unofficial 'national' language; why not Sanskrit?" Panditji fired back.

You tell me, I said to him. *You seem to know.*

"Sanskrit united India culturally, even if only the elite knew it. It preserved our harmony and genius. In order to translate the Bible into every Indian language, Carey mastered Sanskrit and prepared its dictionary. He wasn't serving Sanskrit. His objective was to make it easy for other Bible translators to understand the dialects inspired by

Sanskrit and to turn them into literary languages via Bible translation. Do you know that the Bible is the most translated book in India? It is available in languages which do not have the Vedas, Upanishads, Ramayana or Mahabharata. By developing Indian languages, missionaries divided us linguistically. If scriptures are available in your own mother tongue why would you need a priest who has spent decades mastering Sanskrit? Once priests become irrelevant, so does our sacred culture."

That sounds like unnecessary fear-mongering to me.

"It is necessary to be afraid. You can see the practical consequences of missionary strategy in Sri Lanka, Tamil Nadu, and also Andhra."

What exactly are you referring to?

"Who caused Sri Lanka's terrible civil war? It was European scholars who replaced the notion of Varna (caste) by race. That divided the people into Sinhalese Aryan and Tamil Dravidians. Tamil Nadu is next. I don't know Tamil. It is an ancient language but it does not predate Sanskrit. Missionaries promoted that mischievous idea."

Is it true that missionary-linguists like Robert Caldwell and G.U. Pope developed modern Tamil?

"That is true. They followed Carey but disagreed with his view that Tamil grew independently of Sanskrit. Their strategy was to forge a Dravidian identity in opposition to Aryan. They implied that Sinhalese-speaking Aryans colonised Dravidians in Sri Lanka, just as Sanskrit-speaking Aryans had colonised them in India. Dravidians are revolting now because missionaries taught that the Brahmins had colonised Dravidian culture."

Is this anything serious?

"It is a tectonic fault line. In normal times, fault lines have no practical significance. Eventually, they break apart whole continents. Bengali was the first language that Carey developed. His younger associates, Bible translators such as Henry Martyn in Kanpur, helped make Urdu a literary language. Modern Hindi came later, out of Hindustani, but as a reaction to Urdu. What was the result of these literary developments? Carey's Bengali became the national language of Bangladesh and Sanskrit disappeared from that part of India. Henry Martyn's Urdu rules Pakistan and Sanskrit has disappeared from north-western India. The Hindi that unites north India is not the Eastern dialect, Awadhi, of Tulsidas. It is a language invented by missionaries such as Dr. Gilchrist and Rev. Kellogg. That sadly is Carey's ultimate legacy. In ancient India, Sanskrit preserved our literature, scriptures, and culture. Now it seems destined for the dustbin of history. Even Hindu ashrams in the Himalayas now run English-medium schools not Sanskrit universities."

So did William Carey develop Indian vernaculars in order to divide us along linguistic lines to weaken us?

"I am on my way to England to research his real motives. In public, of course, his followers argue that Europe was reformed when scholars like Wycliffe, Luther, and Tyndale began translating the Bible into the common man's languages such as English and German. They say that you cannot have a government "of the people, for the people, by the people" unless it operates in the language of the people. In the sixteenth century, Paris University in France, Oxford and Cambridge in England, and Wittenberg in Germany, all taught in Latin. Dialects such as French, English, and German had no literature that any university could use. The Bible translators changed that. They enriched vernaculars, making it possible for them to become the languages of learning, law, and governance. That divided Europe even though it made it possible for the common man who did not know Latin to go to college and develop his intellectual potential.

Carey claimed that he was bringing this European linguistic reform to India. His work as a linguist-translator would open up the Indian mind. People would be able to read the scriptures and secular literature in their mother tongues. Imagine—allowing people to read the sacred Vedas or the Gita in a street language, Hindi and Urdu. Carey championed this intellectual revolution to enable people to read and discard the Vedas. How can ignorant masses decide what is true? The Reformers' linguistic strategy undermined the priests' authority in Europe. In India it has been undermining the authority of the Hindu priests. That is a serious attack on Hinduism which depends on a respect for the Hindu priests."

Are you suggesting that Carey developed Indian languages in order to democratise intellectual power? That he made knowledge available to everyone, including low-caste Shudras and women?

"No! Along with his colleagues, he did start the first vernacular college in Serampore that used Bengali as a medium of instruction. It grew into India's first university independent of the British Raj. Carey himself taught astronomy, botany, and forestry—besides languages, and, of course, he taught the Bible. Carey's real motive was to educate us in order to destroy Brahminism and convert us. His faith in the Bible made him such a bigot that he could not appreciate the devotion of the Hindus who sacrificed their children to the Mother goddess. He called it infanticide. That was his first attack on Hinduism."

What else did he do to weaken Brahminism?

"In order to publish the Bible in Indian languages, attack Hinduism, and put pressure on the government to change our traditions, Carey brought the modern press to colonial India—both journalism as well as the printing press. At that time we didn't make the kind of paper needed for the mechanical press, so his mission began manufacturing paper. To mechanise manufacturing, Carey installed a steam engine. That, in turn, started an industrial revolution that weakened our cottage industry. The East India Company had no interest in ushering India into the industrial age. It was a missionary conspiracy to destroy the cottage industry that had made our masses productive."

But did his writing and publishing actually damage India?

"Have you ever wondered why after six decades of Independence, India is still governed by a penal code written by Lord Macaulay? Isn't that enough to show the effectiveness of intellectual colonisation? Macaulay was simply following William Carey who wrote in 1792, one year before coming to India, that the spread of the Gospel would transform India. It will replace the rule of wise men with the kingdom of God. By God's kingdom, Carey meant theocratic laws derived from the Bible."

Panditji, you have said so many new things that my head is spinning. Can you summarise what you are telling me about William Carey?

"I haven't described a fraction of the mischief that William Carey began in the four decades that he spent here. It was not colonialism but Christianity that turned India upside down. If there was no Carey, there would be no missionaries, no Raja Ram Mohan Roy, no Tagores, no Keshab Chandra Sen, no Jyotiba Phule, no Ambedkar, Periyar, or Kanshi Ram. Sanskrit and our sages would have kept India united in one culture. That cultural unity would be much deeper than the political-legal-constitutional unity that the British gave us in line with the Bible's idea of a nation-state."

Vedic India, I said to Mr. Pandit, may have been better than modern India. But from all that you are telling me, it seems that for better or for worse, William Carey, not Mahatma Gandhi, is the Father of the modern Indian nation. Without him, we might have a cultural India but no political India.

"That is true. Even the Buddha was not able to damage Vedic culture as deeply as William Carey did. The Buddha rejected Varna (caste), but he accepted karma/reincarnation as an explanation for self-evident inequality. The Buddha agreed that we are born unequal because of our karma.

William Carey damaged India's traditional culture. Today, it is estimated that at least 100,000 full-time missionaries have come to North India from the South and Northeast. They are transforming grassroots communities where no church existed. Like Carey, many of them also serve the poorest of the poor, the lowest of the low. They educate and uplift the downtrodden to try and make them equal to Brahmins. They fire up the hearts of illiterate people with dreams and ambitions that could be exploited by all kinds of disruptive movements. If you think, you will understand that William Carey laid the foundations for breaking India!"

Panditji, I said hesitatingly, *you are a scholar. I am a simple person. But somehow I feel that many Indians would think that the seeds Carey planted were for breaking the prison that kept our people backward. To be honest, even I can't comprehend why you would refer to the Father of Modern India as 'the nastiest Englishman?'*

"Don't worry," Panditji replied with an air of superiority, "our convent-educated intellectuals don't understand our history and the damage done by missionary's conspiracy. But I can explain my point with a simple analogy . . .

"Think of Hinduism as a mighty citadel made of solid stones that enabled Vedic culture to withstand a thousand years of external aggression. William Carey and the missionaries who followed him became the worst invaders because they did not attack us with swords and guns. They followed Jesus' strategy of the seed and a sower."

Can you explain it to me, please? I requested.

"Carey was like a little parrot that brought the fruit of a banyan tree and perched on the walls of our citadel. Other parrots followed him. They dropped those seeds on the wall. Most were eaten up by insects and birds. A few germinated but died without soil or moisture. A few seeds, however, fell in cracks where enough dirt had accumulated. The sun's rays did not penetrate deep enough to dry up the moisture. Those dark and inaccessible spots allowed the seeds to take root.

One day a plant appeared, growing out of the wall. It looked too tiny to be taken seriously. The caretakers assumed that the plant would die out during the summer. It did seem to wither but it reappeared during the monsoon. It caused no worries because it was not bigger than before. Its shiny leaves looked pleasant on those barren rocks. We tolerated it because we like greenery.

No one saw the real growth that was taking place out of sight. The roots were wrapping themselves around one rock after another.

Some of the roots eventually struck water and nourishment. Then the plant began to quickly thicken and broaden the cracks. By the time the caretakers decided to pull out the plant, it was too late. It couldn't be uprooted without knocking down the wall. But if they didn't deal with the tree, it would breach the entire citadel.

The missionaries who brought the Bible to India knew that they were bringing a seed that had torn apart the Holy Roman Empire. It had transformed Europe and they were confident that it would demolish the citadel that had kept our culture intact."

But aren't our temples flourishing? Haven't our gurus become superstar celebrities?

"Our gurus and godmen have indeed become wealthy. They can fly around in private jets. Perhaps that is what prevents them from seeing that the walls of their citadel are being breached. The backwards are walking out of the citadel, believing that Hinduism has been their prison. There is a huge demographic shift but no one seems to be noticing it."

Does the last census show any cause for concern?

"That is my point: the census counts the leaves that are visible. It cannot track invisible roots."

What are you seeing that makes you so militant?

"My researchers have just uncovered a conspiracy that will make India unrecognisable within a generation or two"

What's that?

"Some Indian missionaries are preparing to turn every local church, in every village, slum and town, into a university classroom."

That is impossible!

"Not really. Their plan is to follow the Wikipedia model to create a curriculum online. They call it a *BA* in *Nation-building* or BSc in nursing or agriculture. Such high-quality curricula, created by experts from around the world and based on the Bible, will be made available online to everyone. Many universities will be induced to use them. The classes will be held in churches. Every church will be equipped with an Academic Pastor who will invite ten to fifteen students to come to the local church, Monday to Friday, for four years to earn a BA or BSc. The lessons and professors will be online, on DVDs, and in books. Students will be able to use their phones, iPads, and tablets, to take lessons and talk to teachers and experts."

But how can churches offer vocational training?

"The Academic Pastors will place students as interns in local businesses, professionals, and NGOs."

But what about science practicals that require laboratories?

"They plan to contract existing labs in schools, colleges, and industries to build labs for local students."

But surely not all subjects can be taught online?

"Their plan is to encourage students to go to a college for short intensive courses when necessary to study what cannot be taught locally."

So, why is this so dangerous? Won't it lower the cost of education?

"This plan will give enormous manpower to every church. The course will require every student to spend at least two evenings a week serving others. The church will use this massive manpower to serve every slum, every village, and every locality."

So, why should that be a concern?

"Can't you see that every illiterate mother will go to the church in her neighbourhood asking for volunteers to help her children with their homework; every widow will go to the local pastor asking him to send two or three volunteers to fix her roof. A church may be meeting in a mud hall with a thatched roof, but it will become the centre of university-level education and service that fights hunger, poverty, and disease. Their aim is to transform whole communities."

This sounds like a revolution! No wonder you are worried.

"Actually, I can't say that I am worried. There are significant currents developing within the church that could sabotage these conspiracies."

Such as?

"Missionaries such as William Carey established universities, but now most American missions have little interest in higher education. In fact, some have turned against basic literacy. They dislike terms such as *illiterate*. They "honour" illiterate people as "oral learners," and prefer to give them stories, not university degrees."

What brought about this change in missionary strategy?

"Some of their theologians started teaching that their old strategies of transforming oral dialects into literary languages, translating the Bible into languages that no one reads, and then teaching people to read their own vernaculars, delays the coming of God's kingdom. Americans want to speed up God's timetable. They believe that as soon as they finish telling Bible stories to those tribes and castes that have not heard about Jesus Christ, the end of this Kaliyug will come and Jesus himself will return to establish his rule for a thousand years. That would be a wonderful fairytale ending!"

You seem to be happy about this new strategy of Western missions.

"Even illiterate parents know what is good for their children. They want their children educated. The new missionary strategy gives Hindu missions the chance to take over the task of educating illiterate people. We can teach them our sacred Scriptures. There is something else that helps me sleep a little better these days."

What is that?

"Fortunately, Western missionaries are very different now than William Carey's generation. They present Christianity as a story. This is good for us because anyone can see that Hindu stories are so much better than Bible stories. The Gospels have just a few short parables. They are called parables to clarify that they are not true stories. The incidents did not actually happen. Most of the Bible was never written as a story. William Carey's generation read it as real history, not as stories. That is why James Cameron based *Avatar* on the story of Ram, not Jesus.

Earlier missions damaged us because they presented Jesus as the Truth. They branded themselves not as storytellers but as "witnesses" telling the truth, the whole truth, and nothing but the truth. That implied that missionary teachers were bearing witness to the truth while Hindu preachers were storytellers, peddling myths.

Defining the conflict as Truth versus Myth was the single most important factor that enabled Christianity to destroy Greco-Roman mythology. Because of its passion for Truth, Christianity came with universities and claimed that it explores history and geology, physics and chemistry, biology and archaeology because it is committed to pursuing truth. Our myths could not compete against their commitment to truth. Fortunately, their new strategy is a game changer in our favor. A conflict between stories—ours and theirs—suits us."

So, do you mean that, after all, you have no reason to fear?

"No! No! We have an immense challenge before us: These new Indian missionaries who are planning to turn every thatched-roof church into a university classroom are using the latest technology, even though their worldview is old-fashioned. They are as interested in truth as in service. American missions may want to protect our culture, including our illiteracy as oral learning, but these indigenous missionaries have become dangerous. They are unabashedly committed to transforming our culture.

Can you imagine the consequences of every low-caste Shudra getting world-class education in his own village? Once a low-caste follower of Christ is made a "priest" he acquires a dignity that his caste never possessed. Naturally, other untouchables are attracted by his preaching.

We have nothing to fear from American missionaries who teach that upper-caste followers of Jesus should not worship with lower-caste believers. This racism of American Christians fits well with our traditional culture of maintaining caste purity. The problem is with these new Indian missionaries. They are taking the education revolution championed by reformers such as William Carey, Ram Mohan Roy, Alexander Duff, Jyotirao Phule, and Bhimrao Ambedkar to its logical end. They are dangerous because they also carry their coffins on their heads. Jesus turned the classical world upside down because he called his disciples to take up their cross as they go out to make disciples or learners of every person, every tribe, every language group, and every nation."

Panditji, I would love to learn more from you, but you have given me so much information that I now need some time to close my eyes and think about what such an education revolution would do to the Backwards. So, please let me take my leave, namaste.

ACKNOWLEDGMENTS

CHAPTER 1 OF THIS BOOK WAS presented by Vishal Mangalwadi as part of a paper at Wetzlar, Germany, at the conference of the International Christian Media Commission, September 11–15, 1988.

Chapters 2 and 4 are revised versions of papers read, respectively, by Ruth and Vishal Mangalwadi at the William Carey Symposium at the Presbyterian Theological Seminary, DehraDun, U. P., India, October, 1991.

Chapter 3 grew out of Ruth Mangalwadi's lectures at the International Management Team's Conference of Food for the Hungry International at Mombasa, September, 1995.

We are grateful to the organisers of the symposium and the conference for their encouragement and for the opportunity to present this material.

The contents of the last chapter was first published in a book, *Why Are We Backward* by Nivedit Good Books Distributors Pvt Ltd.

For the original research and writing for this book, we are grateful:

• to Mr. Sunil Chatterjee and Dr. and Mrs. J. T. K. Daniel of the Serampore College for their sacrificial assistance and hospitality during our visits to the William Carey Library;

• to Roger and Jane Hedlund, Howard and Jill Wilkins, and Prabhu and Phillipa Guptara for their encouragement;

• to Marietta Smith and Jenny Taylor for editing the manuscript;

• to Ted West, Ruth Unrao, and our older daughter, Nivedit, for their assistance in proofreading;

• to the librarians of the Cambridge Brotherhood at Delhi, the Presbyterian Theological Seminary at Dehradun, the Woodstock

School at Mussoorie, and the Bishop's College at Calcutta for the use of their resources;

• to Albert and Audrey Amritanand and Glenn and Marilyn Miller for their hospitality during our research trips to Calcutta;

• to Darrow Miller for his very helpful Study Guide for chapters 1-5 and to Thomas Daniel for the Study Guide for chapter six.

For this edition, final editing and proof-reading was offered by Thomas Daniel, David Linden, Ashish Alexander, Mrinalini Daliya and Sarahna Daliya.

We are grateful to Praneeth Franklin for designing the book and to Andrew Jerome for production.

CAREY'S BIOGRAPHY

Date of Birth: August 17, 1761.

Place of Birth: Paulers Pury, near Northampton, England.

Grandparents: Peter and Ann Carey. Peter was a weaver who later became a teacher.

Parents: Edmund and Elizabeth Carey. Edmund was also a weaver-turned-schoolmaster.

Education: Home-schooled by his father from age six to age fourteen. Apprenticed as a shoemaker to Clarke Nichols of Piddington, and at the same time taught himself theology, Latin, Greek, and Hebrew. His parents "drilled" the Bible into him. Religious Background: John Warr, a fellow apprentice in the shoemaker's shop, led him to Christ. Thomas Scott's preaching strengthened him in his faith.

Marriages:
1) to Dorothy Plackett on June 10, 1781. She died on December 8, 1807;
2) to Charlotte Rumohr on May 8, 1808. She died on May 30, 1821;
3) to Grace Hughes in 1823. She died in 1835.

Missionary Society: Baptist Missionary Society, founded in England on October 2, 1792.

Influential Writing: An Enquiry into the Obligations of Christians to Use Means for the Conversion of the Heathen (1792).

Travel to India: Arrived in Calcutta November 11, 1793, and never returned to his English homeland.

Before Serampore: Resided in Bandel, Manicktullo, Sunderban, and Malda until January 10, 1800.

Serampore: Arrived in Serampore on January 10, 1800, and made it his headquarters. He preferred to call his mission the "Serampore Mission" instead of the "Baptist Mission."

In Calcutta: Appointed tutor at Fort William College on April 8, 1801, and taught there until May 31, 1830.

Translations: With the help of Indian nationals, translated the entire Bible into Bengali, Oriya, Hindi, Marathi, and Sanskrit. Did partial translations into Punjabi, Pashto, Kashmiri, Telugu, Konkani. Also translated smaller portions of the Bible into twenty-three other languages and dialects.

Children:

1) Ann, 2) Felix, 3) William, 4) Peter, 5) Lucy, 6) Jabez, and 7) Jonathan.

Death: June 9, 1834.

A NOTE

On The Jagannath Festival

The horrors of the Jaggannath festival (anglicised to Juggernaut) are vividly described by Buchanan in his Christian Researches in Asia (quoted by V. Mangalwadi in Missionary Conspiracy: Letters to a Postmodern Hindu).

Budruck, in Orissa, May 30, 1806: We know that we are approaching Juggernaut (and yet we are more than fifty miles from it) by the human bones which we have seen for some days strewed by the way. At this place we have been joined by several large bodies of pilgrims, perhaps 2,000 in number, who have come from various parts of Northern India. Some of them, with whom I have conversed, say, that they have been two months, on their march, travelling slowly in the hottest season of the year, with their wives and children. Some old persons are among them who wish to die at Juggernaut. Numbers of pilgrims die on the road; and their bodies generally remain unburied. On a plain by the river, near the Pilgrim's Caravanserai at this place, there are more than a hundred skulls. The dogs, jackals, and vultures, seem to live here on human prey. The vultures exhibit a shocking tameness. The obscene animals will not leave the body sometimes till we come close to them. This Budruck is a horrible place. Wherever I turn my eyes, I meet death in some shape or other. Surely Juggernaut cannot be worse than Budruck.

Juggernaut, June 18, 1806: I have returned home from witnessing a scene which I shall never forget. At twelve o'clock of this day, being the great day of the feast, the Moloch of Hindostan was brought out of his temple amidst acclamations of hundreds of thousands of his worshippers .... The throne of the idol was placed on a stupendous car or tower, about sixty feet in height, resting on wheels which indented the ground deeply, as they mined slowly under the ponderous machine. Attached to it were six cables, of the size and length of a ship's cable, by which the people drew it along .... After the tower had proceeded some way, a pilgrim announced that he was ready to offer himself a sacrifice to the idol. He laid himself down in the road before the tower, as it was moving along, lying on his face, with his arms stretched forwards. The multitude passed round him, leaving the space clear, and he was crushed to death by the wheels of the tower. A shout of joy was raised to the god. He is said to smile when the libation of the blood is made.

SOURCES

Beck, James R. *Dorothy Carey*. Grand Rapids, Mich.: Baker Book House, 1992.

Bradley, Ian. *The Call to Seriousness: The Evangelical Impact on the Victorians*. New York: Macmillan, 1976.

Carey, S. Pearce. *William Carey*. London: Hodder and Stoughton, 1 824.

illiam. *An Enquiry*. Oxfordshire, England: Baptist Missionary Society, 1991.

Chatterjee, Sunil. (1) *William Carey and His Associates in the Awakening of Bengal*. Calcutta: Rachna Prakashan, 1974. (2) *Hannah Marshman: The First Woman Missionary in India*. Hooghly, India: S. S. Chatterjee, 1987.

Drewery, Mary. *William Carey: Shoemaker and Missionary*. London: Hodder and Stoughton, 1978.

Edwardes, Michael. *A History of India*. New York: Farrar, Straus and Cudahy, 1961.

Farquhar, J. N. *Modern Religious Movements in India*. New York: Macmillan, 1951. Ganguly, Nalin C. Raja Ram Mohun Roy. Calcutta: YMCA Publishing House, 1934.

Jones, Kenneth W. *The New Cambridge History of India*. Cambridge: Cambridge University Press, 1989.

Keyes, Dick. "*Pluralism, Relativism and Tolerance*" in The Seer, No. 7. Mussoorie, U. P., India, Nivedit Good Books, 1991.

Latourette, K. S. *A History of the Expansion of Christianity*. 7 Vols. London: Eyre and Spottiswoode, 1945.

Mangalwadi, Vishal. (1) *India: the Grand Experiment*. Farnham, Surrey, England: Pippa Ran Books, 1997. (2) *Truth and Social Reform*. New Delhi: Nivedit Good Books, 1996. (3) *When the New Age Gets Old: Looking for a Greater Spirituality*. Downers Grove, Ill.: Inter Varsity Press, 1993. (British edition: *In Search Of Self: Beyond the New Age*. London: Hodder and Stoughton, 1992.) (4) *The Missionary Conspiracy: Letters to a Postmodern Hindu*. New Delhi: Nivedit Good Books, 1995.

Narasimhan, Shakuntala. *Sati*. New Delhi: Viking, 1990.

Oddie, G. A. *Social Protest in India*. New Delhi: Monohar, 1979.

O'Hanlon, Rosalind. *Caste, Conflict and Ideology: Mahatma Jotirao Phule and Low Caste Protest in Nineteenth-Century Western India*. Cambridge: Cambridge University Press, 1985.

Oussoren, A. H. *William Carey: Especially His Missionary Principles*. Leiden, Netherlands: A. W. Sijthoff, 1945.

Piggin, Stuart, and John Roxborough. *The St. Andrews Seven*. Edinburgh: Banner of Truth Trust, 1985.

Pollock, John. *Wilberforce*. Herts: Lion, 1977.

Potts, E. D. *British Baptist Missionaries in India 1793–1837: The History of Serampore and Its Mission*. Cambridge: Cambridge University Press, 1967.

Schaeffer, Francis A. *A Christian Manifesto*, in The Complete Works of Francis Schaeffer, Vol. 5. Wheaton, Ill.: Crossway Books; 1982.

Smith, George. (1) *The Life of William Carey*. London: John Murray, 1887. (2) *The Life of Alexander Duff*. London: Hodder and Stoughton, 1 879.

Stewart, William. *The Plan and the Sequel: The Missionary Purpose and Legacy of William Carey and Alexander Duff*. Serampore, Hooghly, India: Council of Serampore College, 1980.

STUDY GUIDE

By Darrow L. Miller and Thomas Daniel

As Vice-President of Food for the Hungry International, I recognised the importance of this book for our staff as well as for others who live and labour among the poor and hungry or who are involved in other Christian ministries. My hope is that this study guide will enable readers to reflect more deeply and personally on the importance of William Carey's life for our own time. Please feel free to make a separate copy of these study guide pages, if you so desire.

CHAPTER 1

Who was William Carey? What did he believe? What values and behaviours stemmed from those beliefs and what impact did they have on India? In contrast, what are the beliefs and values of folk Hinduism and what are their consequences in the material world?

1. For three student monologues of your choosing (from chapter 1), use the following charts to identify the beliefs, values, behaviour, and consequences of both William Carey and his host folk Hindu culture. I have illustrated what this might look like for the Science student. The objective here is to begin to see the practical relationship between beliefs and behaviour.

Student of Science: (Example)

	William Carey	Hinduism
Beliefs	*Creation is created; it is good.*	*Nature is "maya"/ illusion. "All is one."*
Values	*All works praise Your name. Nature worthy of study. Insects are created worthy of our attention.*	*Nature is to be shunned. Insects are souls in bondage, and are as valuable as humans.*

| Behaviour | *Meticulously observed Plants. Brought new plants to India. Published books and lectured on science.* | *Forbade destroying pests that eat grain.* |
| Consequences | *Increased interest in science and food production.* | *Decreased food supplies.* |

Student of _____ :

	William Carey	Hinduism
Beliefs		
Values		
Behaviour		
Consequences		

Student of _____ :

	William Carey	Hinduism
Beliefs		
Values		
Behaviour		
Consequences		

Student of _____ :

	William Carey	Hinduism
Beliefs		
Values		
Behaviour		
Consequences		

2. In your own words, who was William Carey?

3. If you had an impression of him before you read this chapter, has that perception changed?

4. William Carey was principle-centered in his development work. Articulate one to three principles that were important for Carey.

5. What did you learn about the importance of a belief system for a people's values. and behaviour, and about the consequences of such beliefs?

6. Why is it important to disciple nations at the level of their practical belief system?

CHAPTER 2

We tend to accept the materialist's paradigm of reality, and analyse poverty from a non-theological perspective. William Carey saw and acted through a biblical set of glasses.

1. According to Ruth Mangalwadi, what created the physical poverty for the women of Calcutta? (pp. 21–39)

2. In his letter to John Williams (p. 21) Carey wrote, "But a people can hardly be better than their gods." This parallels Psalm 115: 1–8, where the psalmist discusses idolatry and concludes, "Those who make them will be like them." How did Carey see this demonstrated in India? (pp. 22–25)

3. What do you think is meant by "false principles"? (p. 19)

4. False principles enslave individuals and whole cultures. How has sin enslaved Hindu culture? (pp. 21–27) Give specific examples of how the belief system impoverished Indian women.

5. Think of your own cultural context. What practices do you see that have been harmful to women?

6. What "false principles" lie behind these practices?

7. What was Carey's strategy for freeing women from poverty? (pp. 34–39)

8. What biblical principles was Carey operating from?

9. How can Carey's insights and methodology be applied to facilitate development in the communities where you work?

10. What is the role of Scripture in setting people free from poverty? What is the foundation for true freedom (pp. 35–46)? Where does development begin?

11. Illustrate how your team currently is or could be consciously using Scripture to lay a "theological foundation for a belief in the sacredness of human life"? How would you expect this to impact the communities where you are working?

12. What, if any, are the implications for you in the community where you live?

CHAPTER 3

We are reminded that it is through the cracks in the clay jar that the light emanates. Identify one or two "cracks" in your life. How does or how can God shine His light through those cracks?

1. What was Dorothy Carey's "sacrifice"? (pp. 41–46) If you could have given William Carey one piece of godly counsel concerning his marriage and life's work, what would it have been? Write a proverb or define a principle that captures the essence of Dorothy Carey's story.

2. What is a "soulmate"? (pp. 47–49) Carey knew a marriage both with and without a soulmate. How does a marriage with a soulmate contribute to Christian maturity? How can a marriage without a soulmate contribute to Christian maturity?

3. How did Carey work to balance his life between being active and being reflective? (pp. 49–52) How is the balance in your life? How do you use your leisure time? What issues are you willing to work on to become more mature in this area of your life?

4. Have you had a loss in your life like Carey's (pp. 53–56)? If you have, please describe it. How did you respond? What did God teach you through the loss? What can we learn from Carey's response to the destruction of his "life's work"?

5. Where did Carey face some of his greatest challenges? (pp. 57–61) What do you think he contributed to these conflicts? What can you learn from Carey's response to these conflicts? Identify a person with whom you have a conflict. What could you do or what attitude could you exhibit that would help restore the relationship?

CHAPTER 4

1. In general, what was the British attitude toward India in Carey's day? (pp. 64–65)

2. How was the reformers' attitude different? (pp. 66–70)

3. Describe Carey's understanding of the relationship between the Gospel and social and economic development (pp. 66–94)

4. What are the implications of this understanding for people who live and work among the poor?

5. What three presuppositions guided Carey's work? (pp. 72–74?) In each case, how does this apply to the transformation of poverty into bounty? All peoples are storytellers. All cultures have their own worldview about what is real and how the world works. If a society is to be transformed, society's "world-and-life view" must be transformed. While William Carey was working to change the "cultural myth" of Hinduism in India, William Wilberforce and Charles Grant were

working to change the outlook in the British Parliament and the East India Company.

6. Changing the belief-system: What cultural myths contribute to moral, intellectual, spiritual, social, or physical poverty in your community or nation?

7. Give an illustration of how you could begin to change the worldview in your community.

CHAPTER 5

1. What is the central thesis of this chapter?

2. Why is it important to examine one's theological assumptions or basic belief system?

3. Why is it important to examine the basic belief system of the people in a community?

4. Let's examine William Carey's basic belief system and its importance for community development or discipling.
a. What was Carey's basic belief about each of the following?
b. What is the importance of this basic belief for community development?
God (pp. 115–116)
a.
b.
Human Beings (pp. 104–111)
a.
b.
The Calling of Individuals (pp. 116–119)
a.
b.
The Church (pp. 119–121)

a.

b.

The Gospel (pp. 212–123)

a.

b.

CHAPTER 6 (by Daniel Thomas)

This chapter is a conversation between a composite character, Mr. Pandit, and Vishal. Mr. Pandit who is apparently traveling to research William Carey, seems to know almost everything there is to know about Carey! He is actually kicking against the truth that he knows. Do you think that his research will unearth anything that goes against all that he knows? Try to use the following questions to apply the insights of this chapter in your encounters with people like Mr. Pandit.

1. What mistake does Mr. Pandit make in equating Carey's profession as a cobbler and those born into the cobbler caste (chamar) in India?

2. "European scholars misconstrued Varna and Jati as caste", Mr. Pandit seems to suggest. Even if this allegation were true, what practical difference does it make? Would it be possible for an Indian born as a chamar to become someone else, without the 'mis-translation' as Mr. Pandit claims?

3. Without the "biblical 'myth' of equality of all human beings", the explanation of inequality provided by Evolution and the Indian sages and even the Buddha would prevail. Would these latter explanations create the modern world that values equality of all human beings under the law and in every other manner? If not then why not?

4. If Carey had not attempted to change cultural practices such as Sati and Infanticide, how do you think these practices would have stopped? If all cultural practices are sacrosanct, should a Hindu Rashtra revive them?

5. To what extent was Raja Rammohan Roy influenced by William Carey to advocate reform of "social evils"?

6. How did William Carey succeed in democratising intellectual power? What is the European model for such empowerment of the common man?

7. The bible is available in all major Indian vernaculars whereas the Hindu scriptures are not available in most Indian languages. Why didn't Hindu Pandits attempt to translate their scriptures into the common man's language?

8. Discuss how does God's word in the mind of the common man threatens the grip of the priestly class on society?

9. "Carey's real aim was to weaken the hold of Brahminism", alleges Mr. Pandit. Was this a noble aim? Discuss.

10. Discuss the impact of the printing press and journalism that Carey's mission introduced on the development of India into a modern nation.

11. "Without Carey there would be no Tagore, no KC Sen, Jyotiba Phule, Ambedkar etc." Is this claim valid?

12. "Cultural unity is deeper than politico/legal unity", says Mr. Pandit. Do you agree?

13. What in Mr. Pandit's view was Carey's strategy to pull down the citadel that safeguarded traditional culture?

14. Have modern mission strategies abandoned the classical missionary conviction of the primacy of truth that would set peoples free? How and why is this so? How do we recover the emphasis on truth in modern missions?

15. How do you assess the effectiveness of the strategy of the "every church in village and city doubling up as a place of learning"? How do

you think this will contribute to the strengthening of the modern nation of India.

16. What prevents Indian scholars from acknowledging that William Carey is the father of "modern" India.

17. Have you met people that hold all or some of Mr. Pandit's perspective on the impact of the gospel on modern India? How do you plan to use this chapter and this book to correct their misunderstanding?

OVERVIEW: What have you learned about William Carey, "the father of modern India"? How has your thinking about missions and development changed? List five ways your insights from this book will help you better achieve your ministry goals.

INDEX

160

ABOUT THE AUTHORS

IN 1987 IN INDIA, ROOP KANWAR, an eighteen-year-old upper-caste Hindu widow, was burned alive on her husband's funeral pyre. Hundreds of thousands of Hindus celebrated this revival of sati, the ancient Hindu tradition that had been banned in 1829 as a result of William Carey's initiative. The incident challenged Vishal and Ruth Mangalwadi, Indians by birth, to explore and apply the spiritual resources of William Carey to initiate a fresh battle for India's regeneration.

Before their marriage in 1975, Vishal and Ruth received master's degrees in philosophy and theology respectively. Vishal studied under Francis Schaeffer in Switzerland, while Ruth graduated from Wheaton College.

From 1976–83 the Mangalwadis lived and worked with the rural poor in central India. In 1984 Vishal became involved in national politics and social reform, organising and seeking to empower untouchables and other impoverished peasants.

From 1987–97 the Mangalwadis lived in and worked from Mussoorie, a hill station in the Himalayas. Since then they have traveled and lectured around the world. Vishal has authored/co-authored 25 books on religion and culture (see list, page 166–167). Currently he is pioneering The Third Education Revolution which aims to redeem education by making it a ministry of the Church to fill the earth with the knowledge of Truth.

Other Books By Vishal Mangalwadi

1. India: The Grand Experiment
(How Victorian Evangelicalism created modern India)

2. Missionary Conspiracy: Letters To A Postmodern Hindu
(Letters to Arun Shourie)

3. Why Are We Backward?
(Roots, Myths and True Hope for Development)

4. The Quest For Freedom and Dignity: Caste, Conversion and Cultural Revolution

5. The World of Gurus
(A philosophical study of the gurus from the 1960's to the – 80's)

6. Conversion: The Revolution India Needs

7. The Book That Made Your World: How The Bible Created The Soul of Western Civilisation

8. This Book Changed Everything: The Bible's Amazing Impact On Our World

9. The Bible in India

10. Truth and Transformation: A Manifesto For Ailing Nations

11. When The New Age Gets Old: Looking For A Greater Spirituality

12. Astrology: Are We Made In The Image Of Our Stars

13. Why Must You Convert?

14. Spirituality of Hate: A Futuristic Perspective on Indo–Pakistan Conict

15. Obama, The Presidency and the Bible

16. The Third Education Revolution
(Editor and Co-author)

17. Dear Rajan: Letter to a New Believers

18. What Liberates A Woman: The Story of Pandita Ramabai - A Builder of Modern India (Main author Nicol MacNicol)

19. Corruption Vs True Spirituality
(Main author Francis Schaefer)

20. <u>Fascism: Modern and Postmodern</u>
(Main author Gene Edward Veith)

21. <u>The Gospel and the Plough</u>
(Main author Sam Higginbottom)

22. <u>Don't Let Schooling Stand In The Way of Education</u>
(Main author Darrow L. Miller)

23. <u>Burnt Alive: The Stains and the God They Loved</u>
(with Babu Verghese, Vijay Martis and others)

24. <u>Healing the Open Wounds of Islam</u>
(An abridged German edition has been published. The English language edition is in the pipeline.)

25. <u>GIRL: Abort or Empower Her</u>
(With Ruth Mangalwadi)